MENTORING & COACHING TIPS

How Educators Can Help Each Other

Sheryn Waterman

Routledge
Taylor & Francis Group
New York London

First published 2013 by Eye On Education

Published 2013 by Routledge
711 Third Avenue, New York, NY 10017, USA
2 Park Square, Milton Park, Abingdon, Oxon OX14 4RN

Routledge is an imprint of the Taylor & Francis Group, an informa business

Library of Congress Cataloging-in-Publication Data

Waterman, Sheryn Spencer.
Mentoring and coaching tips : how educators can help each other / Sheryn Waterman.
p. cm.
Includes bibliographical references.
ISBN 978-1-59667-230-7
1. Mentoring in education. 2. Teachers--Training of. I. Title.
LB1731.4.W37 2012
371.102--dc23

2012030544

Cover Designer: Knoll Gilbert

ISBN: 978-1-596-67230-7 (pbk)

Also Available from Eye On Education

Communicate and Motivate:
The School Leader's Guide to Effective Communication
Shelly Arneson

162 Keys to School Success:
Be the Best, Hire the Best, Train, Inspire, and Retain the Best
Franklin P. Schargel

Creating School Cultures That Embrace Learning:
What Successful Leaders Do
Tony Thacker, John S. Bell, & Franklin P. Schargel

Motivating and Inspiring Teachers (2nd Edition):
The Educational Leader's Guide for Building Staff Morale
Todd Whitaker, Beth Whitaker, & Dale Lumpa

Schools Where Teachers Lead: What Successful Leaders Do
John S. Bell, Tony Thacker, & Franklin P. Schargel

Formative Assessments in a Professional Learning Community
Todd Stanley & Betsy Moore

Professional Learning Communities:
An Implementation Guide and Toolkit
Kathleen A. Foord & Jean M. Haar

Leadership Connectors:
Six Keys to Developing Relationship in Schools
Phyllis Ann Hensley & LaVern Burmeister

101 "Answers" for New Teachers and Their Mentors (2nd Edition):
Effective Teaching Tips for Daily Classroom Use
Annette L. Breaux

50 Ways to Improve Student Behavior:
Simple Solutions to Complex Challenges
Annette L. Breaux & Todd Whitaker

How The Best Teachers Avoid the 20 Most Common Teaching Mistakes
Elizabeth Breaux

Seven Simple Secrets: What the BEST Teachers Know and Do!
Annette L. Breaux & Todd Whitaker

About the Author

Sheryn Spencer Waterman is a consultant and Licensed Professional Counselor. She received a Ph.D. in Educational Studies from the University of North Carolina at Greensboro in 2011. As an Eye On Education author, she has written several books on curriculum design, differentiation, assessment, literacy, and mentoring.

Among Waterman's many accomplishments, she has been honored as "Teacher of the Year" in two schools and received National Board Certification (renewed, 2007). She was a Founding Fellow for the Teachers' Network Leadership Institute and a member of the Board of Directors for the North Carolina Center for the Advancement of Teachers (NCCAT).

She is currently working as a part-time consultant with the Bunnelle Foundation in Georgetown County South Carolina. She is highly interested in the complex nature of helping and the manner in which individuals and organizations offer it and receive it.

Supplemental Downloads

Many of the tools discussed and displayed in this book are also available on the Routledge website as Adobe Acrobat files. Permission has been granted to purchasers of this book to download these tools and print them.

You can access these downloads by visiting www.routledge.com/9781596672307 and click on the Free Downloads tab.

Index of Free Downloads

Contents

Introduction

A novice sent an email to his faculty asking them to help him, but no one responded. He felt so hurt by the negative response that he left before the end of the school year (Waterman, 2012). This is an example of what can happen to a new teacher who is left to his own devices.

Many intelligent and talented people are choosing teaching as a career. Unfortunately, most new teachers have little experience with the kinds of students who need them most and limited ideas about how to function in a school environment. We are losing some of our best and brightest teachers. I have known many idealistic, well-educated, and highly motivated teachers who could not make it in the school system. As a researcher, I have learned some alarming statistics:

- Nearly one fourth of teachers in their first three years of teaching (i.e., novice teachers) either transfer from their schools or leave the profession altogether (National Center for Education Statistics, 2010).
- Studies have shown that nearly one half of teachers leave prior to the fifth year of teaching and the percentage is even higher for schools in rural and low-income areas (National Commission on Teaching and America's Future, 2002).
- The cost of teacher turnover is considerable. For example, Chicago Public Schools lost $15,325 for *each* teacher who left the school system (Barnes, Crowe, & Shaefer, 2007).

Teacher turnover is not only costly, but it also has an adverse effect on student achievement (Terry & Kritsonis, 2008). Even though unemployment is a serious problem, the economic downturn in 2008 has not stopped the constant exodus of teachers from the profession. In an attempt to improve schools, educators from the classroom level to those who help develop educational policy for the entire country are addressing teacher turnover.

This Book Is for All Educators

Since the early 1980s, educational researchers and decision makers have examined mentoring and coaching programs that they believe might help keep teachers in the profession and help new or struggling teachers improve student achievement. Several researchers found that both mentoring and coaching could make a difference. Beginning in 2000, however, studies that challenged those positive findings have emerged. Some have shown that the roles of mentors and coaches have not been clearly defined. In other studies, researchers found that mentoring and coaching made no statistically significant difference as strategies to address retention and student achievement. In response, many schools eliminated some kinds of teacher helpers; most educators continue to believe, however, that new and struggling teachers need help (Waterman & He, 2011).

This book is for *all* educators (including novices) and educational decision makers because it offers tips for how we *all* might help each other. I believe that a combination of mutuality and hierarchy form the basis of mentoring and coaching processes. *All* educators can provide mentoring and coaching services to each other. Schools do not have to spend a great deal of money on full-time mentors/coaches to perform these natural processes. As a matter of fact, those full-time mentors and coaches who have offices and the freedom to manage their own time may find it challenging to be accepted by faculty members. They should take special care to avoid alienating their fellow teachers with their additional power and privileges.

My Experiences

As an experienced teacher, mentor, and coach, I have seen many examples of educators at all levels of our profession who needed help. I wanted to find out more about what might help them. When I left the classroom and became a full-time teacher-helper (e.g., academic facilitator, mentor, and coach), I took advantage of many professional development sessions in which expert trainers asserted that I would be successful if I applied their techniques. The range of perspectives, strategies, and techniques was staggering and often confusing.

Some strategies were useful concepts. For instance, it made sense for specially hired and highly trained mentors/coaches to make learning contracts with teachers, to formally observe them, to conduct pre- and post-conferences about these observations, and to model lessons; in essence, to respectfully guide them toward improving their practices. These strategies all made sense as I was learning them; however, when I attempted to put them into practice, I was disappointed. When I decided to pursue a Ph.D. in curriculum and instruction, I decided to focus on mentoring and coaching. I hoped to discover how educators could most effectively help each other.

A Culture of Helping

I base this book on my several years of personal experience as a helping professional, first as a psychotherapist in the field of mental health, and then as an academic facilitator, mentor, and coach in public schools. Finally I base this book on my graduate work (2007–2011) which included my dissertation. With this book, I have tried to apply this experience and to pose some interesting ways of thinking about how educators might help each other to establish a "culture of helping" in order to improve schools.

Complex Conversations

In this culture of helping, peer helpers differ from traditional coaches and mentors, and traditional hierarchies of advice and evaluation become "complex conversations" (Pratt, 2008, p. 125). These conversations depend on the inclusion of multiple perspectives, the posing of generative questions, and the extension of ideas beyond the expected. According to Pratt, complex conversations are about sharing understanding through community relationships, not about complying with one person's dominant perspective. They involve asking questions, but not the kinds of questions to which we already know the answers. In Chapter 2, I provide details about these kinds of conversations. Many of the tips I suggest in subsequent chapters describe how to use complex conversations, which can be crucial for building a community of helpers. I will provide more explanations and examples to help clarify how to use these conversations. I believe that if educators are willing to change the way they talk to each other (and to their students and parents), they have the potential to change competitive and adversarial cultures into cultures of helping.

There are many other ways that educators can help each other beyond engaging in complex conversations. Before examining these, it is important to understand why some people may not acknowledge that they need help, and why those who do need help sometimes avoid asking for it.

Why People Sometimes Avoid Asking for Help

Help-seeking and support form the basis for mentoring and coaching, but these processes are not well understood. Citing the example of the unfortunate incident of the Hubble Space Telescope, which was initially flawed because the construction team did not seek available help, psychologist Fiona Lee (1997) raised questions about why people avoid help. Lee and many other researchers have confirmed that people may be more inclined to ask for help if they feel that their helpers are their equals (i.e., their peers) in terms of power. Lee insinuated that the Hubble construction team may have failed because, although they may have had experts there to help them, they may not have had *peers* to help them.

Are Mentors and Coaches *Peer* Helpers?

The first mentor, described by Homer, was a wise old man who helped Odysseus's son, Telemachus. Mentor, obviously, was not Telemachus's peer or equal. Today, the relationship between mentors and their charges is a different animal; the dominant perspective has transformed it into a relationship between equals. Although mentors and coaches have roles that differ from those of novices and struggling teachers, all are equals who deserve equal respect. The mentor's power in the relationship is based on superior experience as a teacher, but this should not exceed the power of a novice who may have superior technology skills and more current content knowledge.

Compared to mentoring, coaching is a relatively new idea in the realm of educational reform. In the early 1980s, Joyce and Showers (1983) created studies that promoted coaching as the most successful means of transferring professional learning into classrooms. Joyce and Showers made the point that this successful means of embedded professional development was among *peers*.

Schools have increasingly incorporated mentoring in their induction programs for new teachers, and some have also included coaches to help all teachers improve their practices. In some schools, coaching and mentoring roles might be quite different, and in others they might be indistinguishable. Some believe that mentors should coach new teachers so that coaching as a process involves helping a teacher improve. Others believe that mentoring is more about nurture and support for new teachers, whereas coaches help all teachers. Regardless of how one understands these two roles, they are both described in theory as forms of peer helping.

Researchers seem to agree that mutual respect and appreciation between peers is an important aspect of helping relationships; therefore, we can infer that help from peers can be useful for new and struggling teachers. Unfortunately, even though educators appear to accept the importance of helping each other as an action between equals or peers, program implementation can easily drift away from a peer or equal-power model.

When Mentors and Coaches Are *Not* Peer Helpers

Although researchers and practitioners often define mentoring and coaching as collaboration between equals, program implementation may not align with this accepted definition. The problem is that instructional coaching or technical coaching can promote what some researchers call "contrived congeniality" (Hargreaves & Dawe, 1990, p. 227). Furthermore, Hargreaves (2002) explained that when educators attempt to collaborate through sharing ideas and tasks, the issue of trust becomes extremely important. If trust building is not emphasized, a sense of "betrayal" can deeply affect not only specific helping relationships (p. 393) but also undermine the entire culture of the school. If mentors and coaches do function as peer helpers, I wondered if the claims of research were correct that peer helping could actually make a difference in schools.

Peer Helpers Can Change Teachers' Practices

Most researchers and practitioners assume that teachers' practices have a better chance of improving, and they are more likely to stay in the profession, if schools have mentors and coaches who work with them closely on a day-to-day basis. As collaborative professional developers, school leaders expect mentors and coaches to work as change agents in their schools; however, it is not always clear how they might do that. Some teachers do not welcome change agents, and some are not concerned about their practices. Many agree that changing a teacher's practices and change in general is a highly complex process. Some researchers and educators have noted that schools as complex systems are different from other types of systems, such as simple and complicated ones. In order to better understand the nature of complexity, I primarily consulted the work of the work of Davis and Sumara (2006), who helped me better understand the differences among simple, complicated, and complex systems.

Simple, Complicated, and Complex Systems

These three types of systems are very different. A simple system is like a music box with a toy dancer inside. When I open it, I can expect to hear one song and see the dancer doing one dance. If the music box is complicated, it might allow me to choose from a variety of songs that match a variety of dances so that the interactions are more difficult to predict; yet, they are predictable. However, if the box is a complex system, the dancer would be a human being and the dance would be unpredictable no matter what music plays. Even if the dancer performed a choreographed dance, each performance would be slightly different so that I could not predict with accuracy or certainty the exact nature of the performance. Helping relationships are complex, and it is impossible to predict precisely how they might turn out. This book offers evidence that is complexity-based and it presents alternatives to viewing helping relationships as simple or complicated. It shows how mentors, coaches, and other educators might help each other *plan for complexity*.

Planning for Complexity in Order to Differentiate Helping Relationships

Planning for complexity might sound paradoxical, but I believe it describes how educators might form a culture of helping in order to improve schools. All educators make plans, from the individual lesson plans that address the needs of students in a classroom to strategic plans that address the needs of an entire state. Planning is important, but it is also important that those who make plans understand what complexity might do to those plans. For example, rather than saying we are going to do something, we might say instead that we are *planning* to do something.

I once heard a wonderful math teacher say, "I can teach it to them, but I can't learn it for them." This teacher recognized the interactive nature of teaching and learning—even when we understand what works for the majority of learners, we also need to be open and flexible to the possibility that it may not work for all of them. In a complex world, our plans cannot *cause* something to happen. Our plans might only act as triggers or disturbances from which unpredictable responses might emerge.

Unfortunately, based on the many "how to" books and professional training sessions about mentoring and coaching, it seems that as a culture we still hold tightly to ideas that certain strategies will work for everyone and in every situation. One of the reasons I became interested in differentiation and have written about it is that I firmly believe "one size" does not fit all when it comes to teaching students, as well as mentoring and coaching. If a person acknowledges that individuals, partners (or dyads), small groups, schools, school districts, and other entities are complex, so that different strategies work for different people and in different settings, then that person might change some beliefs about how to interact with them. This book shows how to *differentiate helping* based on ideas about how complex human systems function from the individual to the organization and beyond.

Complexity and the Development of Trust

One of the most important aspects of mentoring and coaching is the process of developing trust. Looking at the notion of trust through a complexity lens and from personal experience, I propose that trust develops in a nonlinear and unique manner. It does not occur in predictable steps, and all trusting relationships are different. Nevertheless, trust seems to depend a great deal on three things: person to person rapport, communications styles, and school culture. When two teachers (such as a mentor and a novice) meet, they could establish immediate rapport and begin to develop trust; however, in other cases it might take several months for rapport to develop. If rapport never develops, trust never happens. In addition, trust can strengthen, diminish, or disappear when two people learn more about each other through their communication styles. These styles may align so that the teachers understand each other, or they can conflict and lead to misunderstandings, Unresolved misunderstandings can negatively affect trust. Finally, trust is affected by the school culture. If the culture promotes competition for the best positions, teachers might feel the need to protect themselves and to be cautious about whom they trust.

Complex Systems from the Individual to the District and Beyond

An important aspect of complex systems is that they are *nested* in other complex systems. Figure A (page 8) shows graphically the several possible nested complex systems involved in a mentoring/coaching relationship. At the center is an individual teacher, a complex system with brain and body functions that interact in complex ways. Unfortunately, although a great

Figure A Nested Complex Systems from the Individual to the District and Beyond

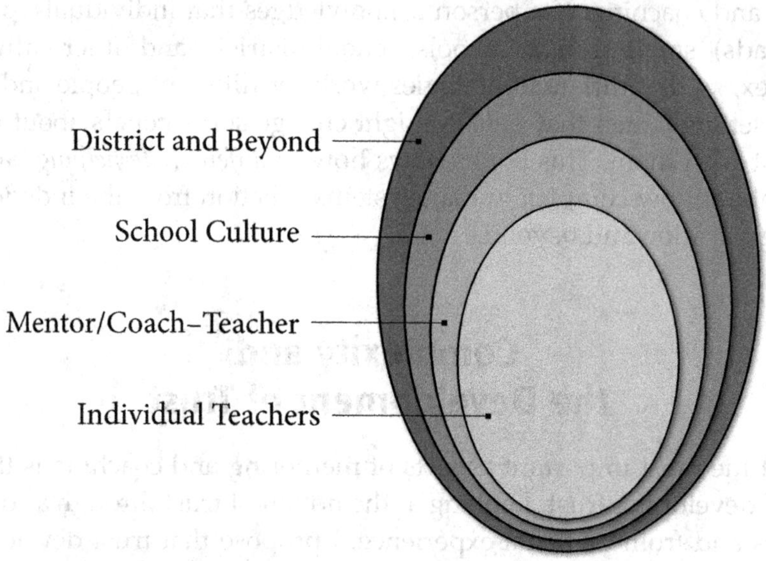

deal has been discovered about the internal workings of individuals (e.g., brain-based research), most of what goes on inside remains a mystery, and we cannot know exactly what a person is thinking or feeling. Therefore, we need to keep in mind that some of our assumptions about what individuals think and feel could be false.

The next level in the nested system is the mentor/coach–teacher dyad. The two-person system is the smallest social system, but it is also complex. The third level is the school culture system, which includes school leaders and other teachers who work in the school. The fourth level is the district level and beyond, which includes all the decision makers at the local, state, and federal levels. All of these levels of the system strongly influence each other. For example, the individual system has a lot to do with how the mentor/coach–teacher dyad functions, and the dyads have a lot to do with how the school culture functions. If we think that any of these levels are immune to actions from other systems we are not planning for complexity or differentiating mentoring/coaching. All of these levels of complex systems are important to all of the other levels.

Collegial Partnerships

In order to make sure that I am sharing ideas useful to mentors, coaches, novices, and struggling teachers without constantly using the awkward designations mentor/coach-novice/struggling teachers, for simplicity's sake, I am going to refer to these four distinct groups as "collegial partnerships" or "collegial partners." In using these terms, I not only avoid awkward word choice but also show that the relationships among these four designations are non-linear and based on mutuality rather than hierarchy. In a culture of helping, the ideas of helper and helpee do not ring true; therefore, note that when I refer to the collegial partnerships or collegial partners, I am speaking about mentors, coaches, novices, and struggling teachers.

How to Use This Book

Educators who plan for complexity in order to differentiate mentoring and coaching acknowledge that learning is a collaborative interaction. When they plan or look at program designs and program implementations, they can determine if those plans allow opportunities for learning to take place in their unique settings. This book delivers the following:

- research findings from a narrative study
- information from the stories that represented the data collected in the study
- tips for implementing ideas from those findings
- time-saving and cost-cutting ideas
- activities that educators might use to implement those ideas

One significant way this book differs from others is that I do not assume that my findings, stories, tips, and activities will apply the same way in every school setting for every mentor, coach, teacher, administrator, and decision maker. I remember being in training sessions which implied that if I implemented a certain teaching, mentoring, or coaching strategy with fidelity, I would get the same results those who were training me had gotten. On many occasions I remember thinking, "This will not work with my students." Or, "This will not work at my school." If I suggested it might not work, the trainers dismissed my concerns and reiterated their claim that these strategies would work anywhere if the teacher, mentor, or coach implemented them correctly. I felt that when the strategy failed, it was my fault. Now I believe differently. I know now that no matter how well a teacher, mentor, or coach might implement a strategy, the unique nature of the school culture and the individuals involved can respond in a variety of ways, including negatively. That is not to deny that personal error may play a role, but mistakes may not have been a factor or the only factor involved in the failure of a strategy. Most important, it is not always useful for individuals to take sole responsibility for or accept the blame for the failure of a strategy.

My hope is that a variety of educators might gather ideas to apply to their own unique situations by reading about how a small sample of collegial partnerships in one school functioned as a complex system to respond to its unique conflicts. Readers might take what applies to them and leave what does not apply. Instead of assuming that what worked for one person in one situation will universally work for others, I invite readers to imagine and adjust the ideas found here to their unique complex situations and to constantly question anyone who suggests that there are simple answers to the complexity of mentoring and coaching teachers. A culture of helping could be useful to us if we are going to educate our students in a complex society. I hope that this book will provide some solid and useful suggestions about how educators might accomplish that goal.

For all future references to the "study" or my "research," unless otherwise mentioned, I am referring to my dissertation (Waterman, 2012). All names of people are pseudonyms, and places have been given fictitious names.

CHAPTER 1

Twelve Tips About Fitting In

Mentors and coaches should help new teachers understand the school culture in order to help them learn to fit in.

School Cultures

When teachers take jobs in schools, even if they worked in the schools as practice teachers, they generally lack substantial understanding of the *school culture,* which includes the beliefs, attitudes, and behaviors of both the adults and the students who interact in the school. It is important to keep in mind that each school has its own unique characteristics and that often it is the mentors and coaches who can help novices or struggling teachers learn to *fit in* with that unique school culture. If teachers fit in, it is more likely that they might stay in a school or in the profession. Some aspects of a school's culture appear to support mentors and coaches in their efforts to help teachers learn to fit in, and some work against them. I will explain each of them and suggest some tips. Figure 1.1 (page 12) is a graphic representation of these factors.

The School Culture I Studied

I chose to study a school that was demographically similar to the schools in which I had been a mentor or coach. These schools are in the southeastern United States and in urban settings. They have challenging student populations, which include large numbers of students from low socioeconomic

Figure 1.1 Supportive and Challenging School Culture Factors Related to Collegial Partnerships

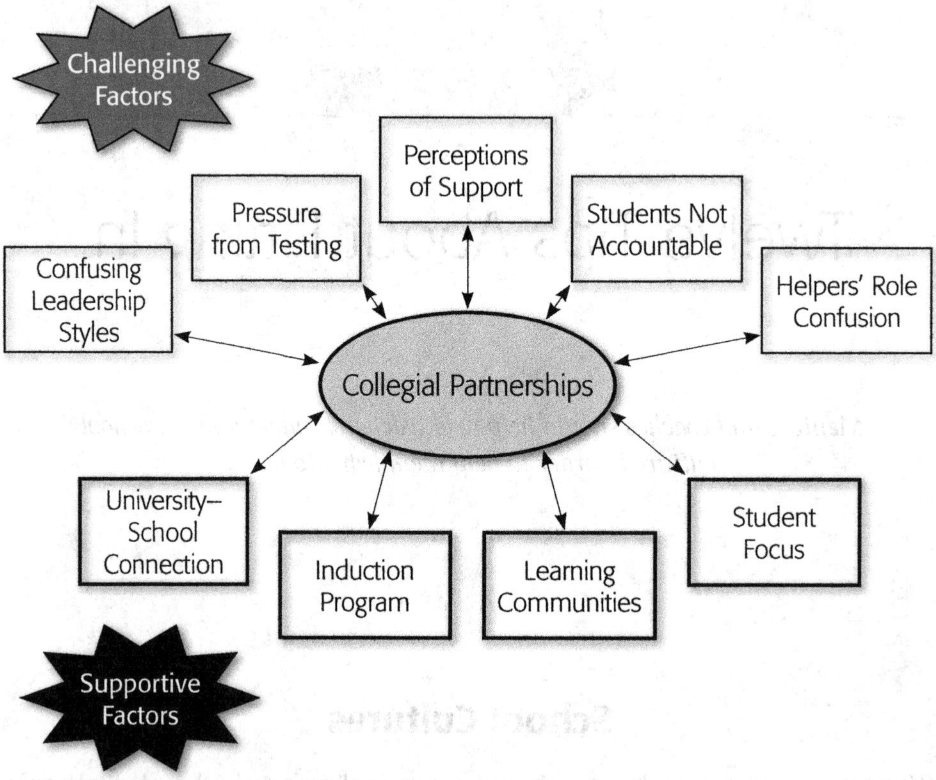

backgrounds, high numbers of low-performing students, and high levels of teacher turnover. I call the school from which I provide real-world examples Lincoln High School. Although I also was a mentor and a coach in middle school settings, I believe this school is highly representative of schools that struggle with teacher turnover; therefore, it provides many useful examples of how colleagues such as mentors and coaches helped teachers deal with many typical school conflicts. It is important to remember, however, that each school culture is unique and no one school or group of schools has the ability to reflect the conflicts of all schools.

Supportive Environmental Factors

The following explanations, examples, and tips address the ways environmental factors can improve the chances that mentors and coaches might help teachers fit in at their schools.

University-School Connection

One of the findings from my research was that the universities that send new teachers to schools to practice teach often play supportive roles and have a great deal of influence on how collegial partnerships work. Sometimes professors who place student teachers in schools have already attempted to match teachers who have a good chance of fitting in at those schools. The most effective professors in charge of school placements seem to have made a point of understanding the school cultures and have made a point of understanding the kinds of teachers who might fit in there.

The Talented Dr. Collins

Some of the mentors I interviewed at Lincoln were impressed with Dr. Collins, the professor from the local university who was in charge of placing student teachers at the school. One reason was that Dr. Collins had made a point of developing a clear understanding of the local schools so that she was able to pair pre-service teachers from the university program with teachers and classrooms in those schools. She had demonstrated the ability to help find teachers that fit well at Lincoln, and the majority of her practice teachers had been successful. Hiring teachers who had practice-taught at the school may not be a common occurrence for other school systems, but it was exceptionally useful at Lincoln.

> **Tip #1:** School leaders, cooperating teachers, and university professors should collaborate to help match pre-service teachers with school cultures. In order to successfully collaborate, school leaders, cooperating teachers, and university professors would cultivate a useful understanding of both the school culture and the pre-service teachers who want to teach in the school. They might then have complex conversations (see "Complex Conversation" in the activities included in this chapter) regarding the fit between pre-service teachers and the school culture. In these conversations, they would welcome and elicit multiple perspectives regarding how novice teachers from the university might adjust to the school culture. These school leaders, cooperating teachers, and university professors might do their best to understand the teacher candidates by using some assessment tools, such as the ones included at the end of this chapter. For example, they may want to know how prospective teachers express caring. By carefully considering each teacher candidate through a collaborative process, they could possibly avoid some costly mismatches. Most importantly, school

leaders may seriously consider including teachers in the hiring process. They might form hiring committees that include those with whom the new teachers will be working.

Many schools are not physically near nor do they have close relationships with the colleges and universities that train their teachers. An idea for establishing closer school-university connections for the purposes of collaboration is to find out where the successful teachers received their teaching degrees. Next, school leaders may develop relationships with those schools through face-to-face, telephone, or virtual communications. Physical distance in the twenty-first century does not need to be the huge barrier it has been in the past. Technology can bring us closer together, and schools might take advantage of technology in order to facilitate closer ties with the universities and colleges that train their teachers.

More Chances to Learn About School Cultures

Another aspect of the university–school connection pertains to whether the school system might provide adequate opportunities for teachers to understand school cultures under "practice" situations. In some systems, universities and state departments of public instruction partner to develop additional internships so that novices not only practice teach at one school but also participate as interns in a variety of settings. In other words, they are not limited to practicing their teaching skills in only one setting and for only one time period. During these internships, university professors help pre-service teachers examine and reflect on their experiences in real school settings. Although these internships do not completely simulate a real teaching position, they do help some teachers better understand the kinds of school settings in which they might best fit; hopefully, they will be able to find jobs in those kinds of schools.

A State Teacher Preparation Program

The state in which I conducted my research had a special program for those teacher education students who qualified to participate. Several of the teachers in my study had participated in this program when they were pre-service teachers. They told me that the program provided not only financial assistance but also additional opportunities for internships in a wide variety of schools in the district. By allowing them to have a more comprehensive view of the kinds of schools available in the district, the program helped my research participants make decisions about the kinds of schools in which they might be successful.

Tip #2: School leaders and university leaders can create additional opportunities (beyond practice teaching for one semester) for pre-service teachers to gain experience in various school settings. School leaders could work with university leaders to set up internships for novices so that they have a wide variety of experience in real schools. However, if a formal internship program is not possible, professors in teacher education programs could include as a class requirement that their students set up their own experiences by applying to a school to do one or all of the following:

- For one day, shadow a teacher who teaches what they intend to teach.
- Volunteer for a semester to tutor a student in a school of their choice.
- Adopt a school for a semester.

Additionally, school leaders could welcome these students from teacher education programs to participate in various activities.

Matching Novices with Cooperating Teachers

Some school leaders are able to hire those pre-service teachers who successfully taught at their schools under the supervision of veteran cooperating teachers. The good relationships student teachers might have developed with their cooperating teachers can be extended and deepened if the cooperating teacher can be assigned as the newly hired teacher's mentor. In most cases, it seems to be a natural transition of roles from practice teacher–cooperating teacher to novice teacher–mentor.

From Cooperating Teacher to Mentor

Two of my research participant pairs, Mrs. Herman (mentor) and Mr. Cook (novice) and Mrs. Rankin (mentor) and Ms. Captain (novice), had previously worked together as cooperating teachers and pre-service teachers. These relationships were productive. Mrs. Rankin believed that her cooperating teacher relationship with Ms. Captain helped them both succeed, and she saw her relationship with Ms. Captain as a partnership. Because Ms. Captain had recently studied their subject in college and was familiar with how to present it using technology, Mrs. Rankin often consulted Ms. Captain about how to teach certain concepts. Ms. Captain also learned a great deal from Mrs. Rankin about how to present content to their challenging students.

Tip #3: School leaders can look for opportunities to hire teachers who were successful practice teachers at their school, and, if the cooperating teacher and the practice teacher had a good relationship, extend that relationship by pairing them as novice and mentor. School leaders could identify these teachers by having complex conversations with the cooperating teacher, the practice teacher, and the university professor, exploring how that teacher might fit in at their school.

Induction Program

The mentoring literature provides many ideas for inducting new teachers into schools. At the beginning of the year before the students arrive, most schools have special professional development sessions for their new and veteran faculty. These sessions acquaint everyone with a wide variety of school and district mandates and policies. Traditionally, various key personnel go over the policies and procedures for which faculty and staff handbooks already provide numerous details. These sessions can be time-consuming, boring, and in some cases intimidating based on the sheer volume of information. Schools might offer special sessions for new faculty only. They might also plan creative interactive events that engage *and* inform new teachers about what it means to be a member of the faculty at the school. These sessions at the beginning of the year say a great deal about the school culture, and they can set the tone for the entire school year. They also provide support to mentors who are trying to help their novices learn to fit into the school culture.

On the Bus

At the beginning of the school year, an event occurred that was highly important to at least one mentor and novice at Lincoln High School. One day, Mr. Hansen took a bus trip with his mentor, Mrs. Truitt. As they traveled through the community where the Lincoln kids lived, Mrs. Truitt told him how she had learned to succeed with their challenging students. Mr. Hansen said that talking to her on that bus trip prepared him for the students who came to him a week later.

Tip #4: School leaders plan interactive induction sessions that present important school and district information in interesting and meaningful ways. (See the activities in this chapter for some specific suggestions.)

Additional Induction Support Before and During the School Year

Although induction programs may provide a variety of services for new teachers, all of them include mentors. Some of the other induction services from Wong (2005) are as follows:

- Support from Administrators: Administrators closely monitor and coordinate programs for new teachers.
- Welcome Center: A place where new teachers can get help to find a place to live, set up their utilities, get maps to important places in the community, and whatever they might need to relocate to their school community.
- Script: The school provides a first-day script to help teachers feel more comfortable. A sample script is at http://teachers.net/gazette/JUN00/covera.html.
- Pre-School Workshop: Provide at least four days of training and team building. This training could help new teachers become immersed in school and district culture.
- Demonstration Classrooms: The school provides monthly opportunities for groups of teachers to observe classes taught by exemplary teachers.
- Networking: Study groups that focus on skill building, problem solving, and team building. Teachers share lessons with each other and build respectful relationships.
- Cooperative Education: Collaboration among a school district, university, and teachers' union in which teachers take workshops and college classes.
- Mentor Training: Mentors receive monthly coaching training sessions throughout the year.
- Long-Term Learning: The school requires new teachers to participate in four years of professional development which included preparation for National Board Certification.
- Multiple Support: New teachers get help from mentors, coaches, and lead teachers.
- Campus Coordinator: New teachers meet on a weekly basis and the meetings are facilitated by an assistant principal.

- Formative Assessment: Before the students arrive at school, beginning teachers participate in at least ten hours of orientation and training about classroom management. Through the year someone guides them to develop the following products:
  - ◊ an individualized learning plan (ILP)
  - ◊ statewide formative assessments
  - ◊ a "Developmental Continuum of Teacher Ability Rubric"
  - ◊ an assessment log
  - ◊ observations
  - ◊ an analysis of student work
  - ◊ a presentation of a portfolio to fellow teachers
- Graduation: Some districts celebrate when new teachers complete the induction period. These celebrations include inspirational speeches, presentations, and a certificate welcoming the novice into the learning community.
- Focus on Student Learning: Induction begins for future teachers at the high-school level and extends through pre-service and into first years of teaching. All training sessions emphasize the importance of developing effective teaching practices that promote student learning.
- Release Time: The school allows new teachers to leave their classrooms in order to observe their peers, attend workshops, participate in peer coaching, and work with "study teams."
- Extensive Training: The school provides training in best practices over new teachers' first three years.
- Socialization and Connecting: The school creates opportunities for time away from school to socialize and connect.
- Full-time Program Coordinator: The school has someone who works with all who are involved (including during the summer) to make sure novices get support.

Source: Wong, 2005, pp. 47–51

Learning Communities

When schools implement learning communities, they increase the possibility of developing a culture of helping. In Chapter 3, I will provide more details about how learning communities function. Basically, they are groups of educators who have common concerns, such as teaching the same subject or the same students, who come together on a regular basis to share ideas, make collaborative decisions, and learn from each other. These communities function best if school leaders value them and provide the time for them to meet. Learning communities support the work of mentors and coaches who are trying to help novices and struggling teachers understand how to fit into the school culture. A learning community structure can provide a place for partnerships to work with other members of their department or team.

Learning Communities at Lincoln

District decision makers mandated that Lincoln High School implement learning communities, and every department had one or more of them. Some research participants felt that community collaborations had helped them, whereas others felt their involvement was a waste of time. School leaders had put content coaches in charge of these communities, and research participants tended to hold them responsible for the success or failure of the communities. In other words, members of the community did not take ownership, and school leaders were not aware of this problem.

> **Tip #5:** One of the best resources for re-culturing schools to include learning communities is Eaker, DuFour, & DuFour (2002). This book provides easy-to-follow ideas about how to shift traditional school cultures of hierarchy and teacher isolation to cultures of shared decision making and teacher collaboration. If a school decides to make a commitment to establishing learning communities as part of the culture, it should also make a commitment to develop a culture of helping that will support collegial partnerships. If a community is struggling with fidelity to the learning community model, complex conversations among school leaders and those involved in that community could help it get back on track.

Student Focus

Collegial partners feel supported when their school cultures value caring for their students. For example, Noddings (2005) concluded that students do best in schools whose teachers show that they care. She distinguished between one-way and two-way caring. In one-way caring, teachers believe they know what is best for students. They show they care by pressuring students do what *the teachers* believe is best for them. Noddings suggested that instead of one-way caring, teachers implement two-way caring in which both the caregiver and the one who is cared for share what the caring process means to each of them, and they mutually care for each other.

Benefit of the Doubt

Mrs. Truitt, a mentor and one of the most successful teachers at Lincoln, modeled two-way caring to encourage student achievement. She believed that teachers and school systems should do their best to understand the needs and abilities of their students and give them the benefit of the doubt when it came to school success. She expressed concern about the devastating effect that failing grades could have on students. Mrs. Truitt suggested that teachers should avoid giving *F*s unless they believed beyond *any doubt* that students had had every opportunity to succeed but had failed to take advantage of those opportunities. Assuming that most students want to be successful and giving them the benefit of the doubt demonstrates a deep sense of two-way caring. It respects individuals' goals and does not imply that teachers and school systems know what is best for all individuals.

> **Tip #6:** In terms of matching teachers with schools, school leaders should determine how faculty and staff view caring. They might use the "How Do You Show You Care?" activity in this chapter to help everyone at the school assess their caring style.

Unsupportive Environmental Factors

Confusing Leadership Styles

For several years researchers have suggested decreasing top-down leadership and making schools more like learning communities where decision making is shared in an atmosphere of mutual respect. Other researchers have promoted the need for more hierarchy and accountability from school leaders, including promoting strict pacing guides and scripted lessons that teach specific standards. In many schools, leaders attempt to accommodate both views, either creating mixed messages and a great deal of confusion or working out fine, depending on your perspective. For example, some teachers like to have structured guidelines proposed in a hierarchical system, but then they close their doors and implement those guidelines in their own creative manner. These teachers have figured out the system and can make a variety of leadership styles work for them. For novice teachers who have not yet figured out the system, however, these mixed messages may create conflicts for them and challenge the mentors and coaches who are trying to help them. Especially difficult are those situations in which leaders put a great deal of pressure on novice teachers and struggling teachers. Unfortunately, these leaders could also be under a great deal of pressure to bring in results so that they pass that pressure down to teachers.

The Right Thing

Mrs. Herman (mentor/coach) provided an example of how the principal at Lincoln, Dr. Thomas, supported teachers who he believed did the right thing for their students. She and all of the other mentors were concerned that everyone at Lincoln was under a great deal of pressure to do what was best for students and to show student achievement. Some novices and struggling teachers did not have the luxury of time to figure out how to make it at Lincoln High School. Sometimes the principal had to make tough decisions and let teachers go who did not seem to fit in at the school.

> **Tip #7:** Mentors and coaches can provide ideas for novices that might improve their understanding about how the school expects them to meet the needs of students. One of the best tips for accomplishing this goal is to use an activity like "Bus Ride."

Pressure from Testing

Although there are many dissenting voices, the dominant attitude about student achievement is that it must be regularly assessed using standardized tests. Many teachers believe that standardized tests measure their success or failure and have learned how to plan instruction based on regular standardized formative assessments. Unfortunately, when tests dominate their evaluation, new and struggling teachers can feel demoralized. Mentors and coaches often have to work against the assumption that teachers whose students perform poorly on standardized tests are failures. There are many strategies mentors and coaches might use to help novices and struggling teachers assess student growth on curriculum objectives.

Bringing in the Stats

Teachers at Lincoln accepted that administrators, district personnel, and other teachers judged their teaching skills based on their students' achievement. However, Mrs. Truitt (mentor) concluded that the credit teachers received for students' scores on End of Grade tests (EOGs) was highly dependent on the level of the students they taught. For example, if teachers taught advanced students, administrators and colleagues gave them little to no credit for those students' scores. However, if traditional or struggling students did well, the teachers received a great deal of credit. If their students did not score well, administrators and the district held them accountable for the students' failures.

Tip #8: Mentors and coaches could help teachers find ways other than standardized tests to capture student growth. For example, they might help novices and struggling teachers use differentiated formative assessments (Waterman, 2010a; Waterman, 2010b). They could also help novices and struggling teachers focus on curriculum standards rather than specific test questions. Finally, they could help these teachers analyze data to inform their practices, look together at student work to determine student achievement, and create common assessments with colleagues who teach the same subjects.

In addition to helping teachers improve instruction that could have an impact on student achievement, mentors and coaches might provide information about the limits of standardized testing, sharing articles such as "Standardized Testing Pros and Cons: Latest Research Analyzed on New ProCon.org Website" (PR Newswire, 2012). Finally, mentors and coaches could help teachers keep students' scores in perspective so that they do not conclude that it was solely their fault if their students failed to perform at high levels.

Perceptions of Support

Educators still use the phrase "sink or swim" to describe the state of support for new and struggling teachers. Although the number of "helpers" has increased steadily since the 1980s, the demands of the job have also increased. This might explain why novices and struggling teachers often feel that they are in a "sink or swim" situation. They often believe that administrators do not support them. When they feel this way, it can be difficult for mentors and coaches to help them adjust their perception.

Sinking or Swimming

Mrs. Baker often relied on the office for support when she had problems controlling her first-semester fourth-period class. Her mentor had encouraged her to develop strategies that would make it unnecessary for her to rely so heavily on the office. By the second semester, she was relying less often on administrators for support; however, she still had the perception in some cases that she was in a "sink or swim" situation. Mr. Manzetti, her mentor, continued to work with her to encourage her to rely more on herself. Mr. Manzetti also believed that administrators had the perception that Mrs. Baker was not growing in her capacity to handle her own classroom discipline, and he knew she needed to demonstrate to them that she was improving.

Tip #9: Mentors and coaches might work collaboratively with administrators and novices or struggling teachers to help them develop positive perceptions about each other. This collaborative work might include scheduling one or more complex conversations that include collegial partners and administrators who are experiencing conflict with each other. All participants in this conversation would make a commitment to the time it might take to answer questions which each person might answer in thoughtful, honest, intelligent, and kind ways. Some possible questions are as follows:

- What contribution is each of us making to the conflict we are experiencing?
- What gifts do each of us have that we have not explored?
- What is the story we keep telling about each other that keeps us in conflict?
- What new story might we tell that moves us toward a shared understanding?

In the cases where novice or struggling teachers have the perception that administrators are against them, it is important that collegial partners keep negative personal communications confidential. However, just promoting the idea that partners should keep information about teachers confidential may not be enough. It is human nature to talk about one's experiences. Mentors and coaches do not always have safe spaces where they might be able to talk to other mentors and coaches about their experiences and the problems they might be having; therefore, they can fall into the trap of trying to solve their problems by betraying confidences.

Tip #10: Recognizing that many collegial partners may need to talk about their experiences and problems, school leaders might create a structure that makes it possible for mentors/coaches to have a safe and confidential setting for sharing and problem solving with colleagues. They might create this safe space by encouraging mentors and coaches to meet during or after school at least once per month to have authentic dialogue about their experiences with novices and struggling teachers. School leaders may strongly suggest that participants in these sessions talk about *situations* rather than *specific people* and that they focus on how events affected them rather than focusing on problem people. They could set some norms that include keeping the

> conversations confidential, talking from the "I" perspective, and sharing ideas rather than giving advice. They could also suggest some protocols such as taking turns leading the meeting, taking turns sharing information, limiting time for sharing, and limiting the time of the meeting to no longer than one hour.

Students Not Accountable

People and policies that do for students what they might do for themselves weaken them and do not do them any favors. On the other hand, some students truly do not have opportunities to learn for various reasons (e.g., trying to learn in chaotic classrooms). Unfortunately, many students do not respond well to certain classrooms or school structures so that they do not truly have opportunities to learn, but in other cases some students who *may* have opportunities to learn choose not to take those opportunities. It is often difficult to determine if students are "playing" the system or if they are victims of it. Sometimes school policies enable students to experience a false sense of success. When teachers have to participate in enabling policies, they can feel that their instruction is undermined. For example, when school policies pass students who fail to attend school or do enough work to convince teachers that they have mastered the objectives of their class, some teachers can feel that their instruction and their work is unimportant. These policies also can generate excessive paperwork and monitoring that can be especially challenging for novices or struggling teachers. Enabling policies can make it difficult for mentors and coaches to help novices and struggling teachers cope with their emotional reactions and also with the physical demands of keeping up with non-compliant students.

Making Problems

School policies that enabled his students to escape accountability bothered Mr. Cook (novice). From his perspective, the huge amount of work these polices created for teachers and the messages they sent to students undermined his effectiveness as a teacher and hurt students. Mr. Cook believed that when education leaders made policies, they were most likely trying to resolve problems, but for him some of the policies created the problems they were trying to resolve. He noticed that some of his students had discovered they could take advantage of a process that allowed them to recover from not doing their work during regular classroom time. He said that at the time decision makers made the policy, some students may have actually needed this kind of process, but that now they were telling the students behind them that they were able to graduate without doing much during the school year.

Tip #11: Mentors/coaches may be able to help novices or struggling teachers provide opportunities for all their students to learn, such as managing classroom disruptions and keeping students interested in attending classes. By helping the majority of their students succeed, they may not have to complete an overwhelming amount of paperwork. Collaborative helpers might also help novices or struggling teachers determine ways to cope with school policies that provide opportunities for students to make up work. Some of these ways include keeping good records about students' opportunities to learn, getting help from parents, not leaving the paperwork until the last minute, implementing classroom contracts with students, and working with other team members to contact parents, contract with students, and complete paperwork.

Helpers' Role Confusion

Sometimes schools have so much teacher turnover that their supply of collaborative helpers is limited. For example, some teachers in my study were both mentors and coaches. One was a mentor, a classroom teacher, and a department chair. In many cases teachers are able to perform many roles, but at times the objectives and standards inherent in one job might interfere with or contradict another. Dual roles can be especially challenging if novices or struggling teachers have limited access to mentors or coaches because they are too busy with their other roles. Occasionally, role expectations can conflict. For example, principals might expect coaches to tell them how certain teachers are performing, and they might expect mentors to provide emotional support without evaluating and reporting novices' performance. School cultures that require mentors and coaches to serve multiple roles can make mentoring and coaching even more challenging.

Not Enough Time to Do Both

In my study, one of the mentors, Mrs. Stanley, was also a part-time content coach, so she was only in the school two days per week. Her limited time and the fact that she was responsible for coaching an entire department made it impossible for her to provide traditional mentoring services to her mentee, Mrs. Lawson. Unfortunately, she was the only person associated with Mrs. Lawson's department who remotely qualified to be her mentor. Mrs. Lawson reported that she found out from a colleague who attended a meeting in which administrators criticized him that much of the negative information about his performance had come from Mrs. Stanley, who was also his coach. Based on the information Mrs. Lawson learned from her colleague, she did not feel comfortable sharing certain information with Mrs. Stanley during their first year together.

An easy solution to pairing Mrs. Lawson with a mentor was not available, and Mrs. Stanley's dual role as mentor and coach was confusing to Mrs. Lawson, especially during the first year when Mrs. Stanley seemed more aligned with administrators than teachers. This example points to the potential problem when coaches and mentors serve dual roles or when they are not sure with whom to align.

> **Tip #12:** Mentors and coaches need to seek clarity about their roles. For example, mentors may have a commitment to one or more novices, and coaches may work with entire teams. Mentors *and* coaches might have complex conversations that establish their equality with novices and struggling teachers and confirm the belief that they both bring valuable knowledge to the relationship. They might also address norms for their relationships, such as how they plan to get together and where, how often they plan to get together, and what kinds of topics they will address. Once they agree upon expectations regarding their roles, they might determine if administrators also agree with those expectations. Novices and struggling teachers should not have to wonder if it is safe to vent frustrations or to show weaknesses to their helpers.

Saving Money and Time

Teacher turnover creates a long list of losses. The costs in time and money are tremendous and can be devastating to a school district, a school, and to individuals who give up on teaching. By acknowledging the complex nature of school cultures, decision makers and practitioners might better anticipate factors that could influence teacher turnover. A critical factor relates to how well teachers fit into certain school cultures. By relying on already existing programs (e.g., teacher education classes and orientation programs), processes (e.g., hiring interviews), and staff (e.g., principals), those who prepare teachers, those who hire and supervise them, and potential teachers might learn to become more aware of the notion of diverse school cultures and finding best matches between teachers and those cultures. Taking steps to avoid errors in matching teachers with schools could save considerable time and money, and it does not take any more money to put these ideas in place.

In the next section, I provide some activities that might help mentors and coaches help novices or struggling teachers discover the school culture and their own styles to determine if the schools and individual teachers are a good match.

Activities

These activities could be useful in group settings or just between mentors and mentees or among coaches and the teachers with whom they work. Note that in several cases I suggest that during these activities participants use *authentic dialogue* (another term for complex conversation) to talk about the ideas that emerge in the activity. By authentic dialogue, I mean honest and candid conversation among equals who are convinced that everyone involved will respect, appreciate, and hold confidential the details of the conversation.

Relationship Builders

The website "Tools for Mentoring" (Father Heart Ministries, 2010) has a wealth of "Relationship Builders for Small Groups." The following are a few ideas and adaptations of ideas from this website:

1. Ways to Introduce Yourself to a Group
    - Introduce yourself as your parents would introduce you.
    - Introduce yourself as if you were a nifty new product.
    - Introduce yourself as your best childhood friend would introduce you.
    - Make an acrostic poem, in which the first letters of your name begin poetic phrases that describe you, and share it with the small group.
    - Create list of what you want to know about the other people in the group (e.g., place of birth, number of siblings, favorite music, heroes, etc.). Members introduce themselves by addressing what is on that list.
    - Tell two things that are true about yourself and one thing that is a lie, and ask group members try to guess which things are true and which is the lie.
2. Ways to Find a Partner. Give each person a card that states a part of two things that match. For example:
    - first and last names of historical figures (History)
    - names of inventors and pictures of their inventions (Science)
    - names of authors and titles of their books (English)
    - math equations and answers (Math)
    - pictures of musical instruments and names of musicians (Music)
3. Ways to Group People. All of the people who have the same thing gather at a table that displays what they all have in common.
    - candy bars or pieces of candy
    - puzzle pieces that make the same puzzle

- leaves that belong to the same type of tree
- same color marbles, paper clips, pencils, markers, or other colorful objects
- same inspirational saying
- same picture of a famous person

4. Ways to Learn Group Members' Names
   - One at a time, group members say their first names and then mime an action that starts with the first letters of their names. The first person starts with his/her name and then the next person says his/her name and the first person's name. Names are added as members go around the circle.
   - Use the same process as above, but toss a ball to determine who goes next instead of going around the circle.
   - Use the same process of sharing names; however, instead of making motions that stand for the first letters of their names, group members mention symbols for themselves (e.g., a pencil for someone who likes to write, a cell phone for someone who likes to communicate) or objects that start with the first letters of their names (e.g., a pencil for Patty, a cell phone for Christy).

5. Ways to Learn More About Group Members
   - This is a variation of musical chairs. Arrange chairs in a circle for everyone in the group and set a chair in the middle of the circle. (Hint: You may want to spread these chairs out quite a bit.) The person who goes first describes something he or she has done and says, "If you have ever ..., then move to another seat. (Example: "If you have ever sung in the shower, move to another seat.") As soon as he or she finishes saying the sentence, everyone who has experienced the activity gets up to move, and the person in the middle also tries to find a chair in the circle. The one left standing becomes "it" and must sit in the middle chair. The game continues for a few more minutes until everyone has had a chance to be "it" a few times.
   - Ask everyone to bring an interesting object to place in a brown paper bag. After all of the objects are in the bag, someone starts by reaching into it and pulling out an object. (It is all right if they get their own object.) The person must then make a statement about what the object means in terms of their lives. For example, if a person pulls a piece of candy out of the bag, he or she might say, "This candy reminds me how sweet it can be to become a member of a group," or, "This candy describes my sweet personality."

Complex Conversations

These are conversations that are useful for pushing through conflict, for changing the status quo, and for creating a sense of a community of helpers. "Differentiating Traditional Conversations from Complex Conversations" is an overview of the differences between traditional and complex conversations.

Differentiating Traditional Conversations from Complex Conversations

Key Factors	Traditional Conversations	Complex Conversations
People involved in the conversations	Limited to those who have the answers and make the decisions	Expanded to include those who wonder about the answers and how decisions might affect them
Knowing/learning relationships within the conversations	Differentiates between those who have information and elevates them above those who receive information (knower–knowee relationships)	Values and equalizes all types of information. Assumes that everyone is a knower and does not differentiate or elevate one above the other.
Questions that the conversations address	Those to which we know typical answers and that maintain the status quo, such as: Why did you become a teacher? (e.g., to make a difference, I like kids)	Inviting questions that elicit commitment and accountability, such as: How valuable do you plan for your participation at this school to be?
Quality of questions	Weak because they have little power to create new directions and change for the future	Powerful because they involve personal commitment, passion, and accountability to create new directions and to change the status quo
Purposes of the conversations	For example: agreeing with the dominant perspective, making plans, analyzing problems, assigning tasks, making decisions	For example: creating space for deep inquiry, making new discoveries, accepting personal responsibility, and exploring possibilities

Source: Adapted from Block (2008) and Pratt (2008).

One of the cornerstones of complex conversations is the quality of the questions. Here are three criteria:

- ♦ They are ambiguous, so they require each person to bring personal understandings into the conversation.
- ♦ They are personal, so they elicit passion, commitment, and connection.
- ♦ They evoke anxiety because they matter to each person. (Block, 2008)

In order to have a complex conversation, the person initiating it needs to take these steps:

- ♦ Invite another person or others to make a personal commitment to share the responsibility for the conversation.
- ♦ Carefully consider the questions that will start the conversation and remain open for new questions to emerge.
- ♦ Agree with those involved that the space is safe for honest and open talk.
- ♦ See what emerges and make a personal commitment to following through with the ideas that emerge.

Bus Ride

Step 1: Take participants on a bus trip around the neighborhoods represented at the school. Have drivers drive around for about half an hour. Do not take too long. It does not take long to get the point.

Step 2: Ask mentors and novices to sit together on the bus.

Step 3: When you return from the bus ride, break into groups of eight to ten. Some leave out this step, but I think this misses an opportunity to begin the process of sharing important information and learning about the students' world.

Step 4: Ask each group to find a leader to be responsible for reading the following questions and allowing comments from all group members:

- ♦ How did the neighborhood compare to the one you grew up in?
- ♦ What did you see people doing in this neighborhood?
- ♦ What kinds of concerns would you have if you lived in this neighborhood?
- ♦ How do you think school work is viewed in this neighborhood?

Step 5: Allow other questions to emerge and make sure to allow enough time for conversations to expand and deepen. Talk for at least one hour, but no more than one and one half hours.

Retreat (One- or Two-Day)

Step 1: Find a place away from the school or have the retreat at the school.

Step 2: Provide drinks, snacks, and meals for everyone.

Step 3: Designate spaces where those who will work most closely with each other can form into teams as they arrive at the retreat.

Step 4: To start the retreat, the leader announces that the purpose of the retreat is that everyone should have a good time participating in team-building and information-gathering activities.

Step 5: Use some of the activities described in this book to make sure teams are built and everyone feels a part of the school culture.

Are We a Match?

This matching activity might be implemented in one of two two ways by pairs (e.g., a mentor and novice), within a small group (e.g., a coach and struggling teachers), or within a larger group (e.g., at a mentoring or coaching training session):

1. The mentor or coach answers the questions in the first column, and the novice or struggling teacher answers the questions in the second column. They decide together if they should circle Y (yes) or N (no) in the third column to determine if the school and teacher match. They can then participate in an authentic dialogue about the findings.
2. The mentor or coach and the teacher answer the questions in both columns, and then circle Y (yes) or N (no) to note if the school and teacher match. They may compare their answers and the conclusions they reached. They can then participate in an authentic dialogue about the findings.

School	Teacher	Match
What is the leadership style of the administrative team (or principal)?	With what kinds of leadership styles is the teacher most comfortable?	Y N
How important is testing accountability at this school?	How important is testing accountability to the teacher?	Y N
Describe the level of pressure teachers deal with at the school.	How well does the teacher work under pressure?	Y N

(continued)

School	Teacher	Match
What kinds of support do teachers get at the school?	What kinds of support does the teacher prefer or need?	Y N
How does the school culture hold students accountable for achieving and behaving?	How does the teacher hold students accountable for achieving and behaving?	Y N
What are the roles of mentors, coaches, and other helpers in the school?	How does the teacher welcome help and support?	Y N
Describe the induction program that supports the work of mentors/coaches.	What have been the teacher's experiences with mentoring and coaching?	Y N
How does the school implement professional learning communities that help teachers better collaborate with each other?	How does the teacher function in professional learning communities?	Y N
How does the school address the needs of difficult students?	How does the teacher address the needs of difficult students?	Y N

Dreams and Dreads

This activity can be used with pre-service, new, or struggling teachers. They might compare their responses with those of their mentors or coaches, who also participate in the activity. Coaches and mentors might learn a great deal about themselves and their current situation by participating, and by sharing as equals, they might help novices and struggling teachers identify some of the challenges they could face or are already facing if they are not working at their "dream schools."

Step 1: Choose one of these ways to describe the school of your dreams.

- Write a descriptive paragraph.
- Draw a picture. Label it to include specific ideas, such as number of students, etc.
- Make a chart or bulleted phrases.
- Create a PowerPoint presentation.
- Write a poem or rap song.

Include some or all of these ideas: location of the school in relationship to where you live, size of the building and number of students who attend, school architectural style (e.g., modern, traditional), when the bell rings, what the students look like, what the classrooms look like, what the fellow teachers look like, what they believe about learning, what you are teaching, how the principal and administrative team function, how your fellow teachers interact, what the parents are like, in what kind of community is the school located, and anything else you believe is important to describe.

Step 2: Share your work.

Step 3: Choose the same way or another way to describe the *school of your nightmares* and include similar factors.

Step 4: Share your work.

Step 5: In an authentic dialogue, participants might draw conclusions about what these descriptions mean, especially if reality dictates that the only jobs might be in schools that do not match their dreams. Important questions this activity could raise are as follows:

- What do you do when your ideals do not match reality?
- How much are you willing to give up in order to work in a school that in many cases does not match your dream?
- What kinds of skills do you need to be able to adjust in a school that you dread?
- What kinds of resources might you utilize to help you adjust?
- What should you do if you find yourself complaining constantly about your situation or if you feel you are not successful?
- What should you do if school leaders, students, parents, and/or your colleagues seem at odds with you?

Learning Styles Checklists

In many cases a school culture will be dominated by certain learning styles, and those who are new in the school may find themselves at odds with others simply because of their learning styles. What follows are two learning styles checklist ideas that mentors might use with their mentees, that coaches might use with struggling teachers, or that induction leaders might use in retreats and training sessions. Using these checklist ideas can also help mentors and coaches find out how well they match novice or struggling teachers.

Four Learning Styles: Sensory-Based

Step 1: Make copies of a "Sensory Styles Checklist" that includes descriptors for those whose sensory styles are one of the following: Auditory, Visual, Kinesthetic, or Tactile. There are many such checklists available in print and online. You can find an excellent list at www.learningabledkids.com/home_school_info/learning_styles.html. Also make copies of the following template, "Mine and My Colleague's Sensory Learning Styles." To save paper, you may want to copy this template at the bottom of your checklist.

Step 2: Label the four corners of the room with the following sensory styles: Auditory, Visual, Kinesthetic, and Tactile. In the middle of the room, place a label that says "Eclectic" (which means no one dominant style). Encourage participants to try to determine their dominant styles, but use "Eclectic" for those who insist that they cannot do it.

Step 3: After all participants have individually completed the checklist to determine their dominant sensory styles, ask them to move to the corresponding corner.

Step 4: When participants are gathered in their corners, ask them to do one of two possible activities: (1) make a collaborative graffiti poster that reflects their dominant style or (2) have a conversation with each other about what it means to have their particular style.

Step 5: Ask groups to pick one or two members to report about their style to the whole group.

Step 6: Ask each participant to fill in the "Mine and My Colleague's Sensory Learning Styles" template by including the name of ***at least*** one colleague in each box.

Mine and My Colleague's Sensory Learning Styles

Auditory	Visual	Kinesthetic	Tactile	Eclectic

Step 7: Tell participants that when they get ready to plan a lesson based on sensory preferences, they might want to get feedback from those whose styles are similar and different from theirs.

Four Learning Styles: Psychology-Based (Carl Jung)

Follow the same steps from "Four Learning Styles: Sensory-Based," but use the "Four Psychology-Based Learning Styles Checklist" below.

Four Psychology-Based Learning Styles Checklist

Mastery Style	Interpersonal Style
Learns best by ___ Seeing concrete evidence ___ Practicing ___ Knowing what to expect ___ Finding "right answers" ___ Doing drills and assignment sheets ___ Knowing exact expectations ___ Getting quick and accurate feedback ___ Being recognized for work well-done ___ Being an active learner ___ Having "hands on" opportunities ___ Seeing what to do (teacher modeling) ___ Getting directions step by step Able to Organize ___	**Learns best by** ___ Seeing how concepts relate to people ___ Working with groups ___ Sharing ideas ___ Getting positive personal attention ___ Role playing ___ Learning about self, especially feeling ___ Bouncing ideas off of someone else ___ Getting feedback from others ___ Collaborating Able to Empathize ___
Understanding Style	**Self-Expressive Style**
Learns best by ___ Analyzing situations ___ Debating or arguing about ideas ___ Working with other understanding-style people ___ Thinking about and studying the relationships among ideas ___ Carrying out interesting projects ___ Solving problems that require inquiry and evaluation Able to Interpret ___	**Learns best by** ___ Multitasking ___ Being creative ___ Working with others on creative ideas ___ Discussing open-ended questions and topics ___ Discovering for myself ___ Thinking outside the box ___ Organizing in my own way Able to create ___

Source: Adapted from Silver, Strong, and Perini (2000, p. 28).
Reprinted with additional adaptations from Waterman (2005, p. 15).

Mine and My Colleague's Psychology-Based Learning Styles

Mastery	Understanding	Interpersonal	Self-expressive	Eclectic

Both of these checklist ideas can start useful authentic dialogue on topics such as:

- What does our faculty believe about how we and our students learn?
- What are the learning styles of the majority of our teachers and staff and how might that affect our school culture?
- How might we best utilize the diverse learning styles we have at our school?
- How might differences in learning styles affect our teaming, co-planning, and problem solving?

Comparing Views of Our Schools

This activity could be useful for mentors and novices and coaches and struggling teachers. It could also be useful in a training session for novices and struggling teachers who are accompanied by their mentors and/or coaches.

Step 1: Give each participant the template "Describing My School and Myself." Tell them that they will have a chance to walk through the school for about ten minutes in order to take notes that will help them write a description of their school. If you use this activity in pairs or in small groups, walk through the school separately and make your notes separately. If you use this in a group training, send out small groups of novices and struggling teachers and other groups of mentors and coaches (in other words, separate the novices and struggling teachers from the mentors and coaches) to walk through the school in order to describe it.

Step 2: When notes are completed, mentors and coaches, along with novices and struggling teachers, will use them to write descriptive paragraphs.

Step 3: Participants take turns sharing their descriptions.

Step 4: Participants record three important similarities in their descriptions and three important differences.

Step 5: Participants describe the people who make up the school (e.g., the students, other teachers, principal). Novices and struggling teachers in some cases may need to describe their assumptions about the people who make up the school. Note that these assumptions could be based on their own school experiences, previous experiences in similar schools during practice teaching, or other involvement in schools.

Step 6: Participants again share their descriptions and record three similarities and three differences in their perspectives.

Step 7: Participants reflect on how they fit in at the school. Then share with each other and again write three similarities and three differences.

<table>
<tr><th colspan="2">Describing My School and Myself</th></tr>
<tr><td colspan="2">What does it look like?</td></tr>
<tr><td>Similarities:
1.
2.
3.</td><td>Differences:
1.
2.
3.</td></tr>
<tr><td colspan="2">Who are the people who come here?</td></tr>
<tr><td>Similarities:
1.
2.
3.</td><td>Differences:
1.
2.
3.</td></tr>
<tr><td colspan="2">How do I fit in?</td></tr>
<tr><td>Similarities:
1.
2.
3.</td><td>Differences:
1.
2.
3.</td></tr>
</table>

This activity should generate authentic dialogue that addresses questions like these:

- Do my views of the school match my mentor's/coach's views?
- Do my views of the school match my novice's or struggling teacher's views?
- What should we do about our different perspectives?
- What are the implications for our views about our school and how we fit in here?

How Do You Show You Care?

This is a self-assessment based on ideas from Noddings (2005). Mentors, coaches, and other helpers might help novices and struggling teachers determine how they show they care for their students. If they compare their caring styles with those of their mentors, coaches, or other teachers and staff, they might get a better sense of how well they fit in at their schools. For example, if the dominant caring style is two-way caring and teachers show one-way caring, then they might run into some problems fitting in.

Put a check in front of the sentences that best describe you. Count the checks in each column and record the total. The side with the most checks indicates your dominant caring style.

One-Way Caring	Two-Way Caring
___ Students often do not know what is best for them, and they need a teacher to advise them about what that might be. ___ Students know I care for them when they do well on important tests. ___ Helping my students achieve success on district or state-determined academic standards is the best way I can show them I care. ___ I am not demonstrating care if I allow students to get away with not doing their work. ___ A caring teacher is one who holds high standards regardless of pressures to lower them. ___ Teachers who care challenge students to overcome the limitations the teacher has found in their work. Total number of checks ___	___ Students tell me what is best for them and I respect their beliefs. ___ I understand that standardized tests can sometimes harm students, and I help students keep them in perspective. ___ Helping students achieve what is important to them is more important than helping them achieve what the school district thinks is important. ___ I recognize that sometimes the work I plan for students does not match their needs, and I can be flexible in terms of my expectations. ___ I feel successful if I am able to help my students achieve their goals, not mine. ___ I believe in the old saw: Students do not care what you know until they know that you care. Total number of checks ___

This activity should generate authentic dialogue that addresses questions like these:

- In what ways does my caring style match my mentor's (or my coach's) style?
- In what ways does my caring style match my novice's (or my struggling teacher's) style?
- In what ways does my caring style match the dominant caring style of school leaders?
- How do teachers at this school show how they care about students?
- What kinds of caring styles are apparent in the policies and procedures in place at this school?
- How does my style of caring match the policies and procedures in place at this school?

CHAPTER 2

Four Tips About Self-Organization

Collegial partners develop their own ways of working together.

Collegial Partner Assignments

Many schools have programs in which mentors and/or coaches are formally assigned to novices and/or struggling teachers. In some schools, novices and struggling teachers find their own mentors and coaches if no one assigns them or if they do not fit well with the assigned person. Regardless of the manner in which mentors and coaches get together with novices and struggling teachers, and regardless of program requirements, it seems that most mentors, coaches, and teachers decide for themselves how they will work together in partnerships. Four factors play roles in self-organization: matching each other, both formal and informal pairing, space for emergence, and the person system. (See Figure 2.1, page 40.)

Matching Each Other

It is important that novices and struggling teachers not only determine how they fit in at their schools but also work well with their assigned mentors and coaches. If they are too much alike, they might not learn from each other, and if they are too different, they may not be able to relate to each other. Mismatches can come from a variety of sources, including having the same weakness (e.g., blind leading the blind) or having personality and philosophical differences. Other mismatching could come from similarities

Figure 2.1 Self-Organized Systems: Four Factors

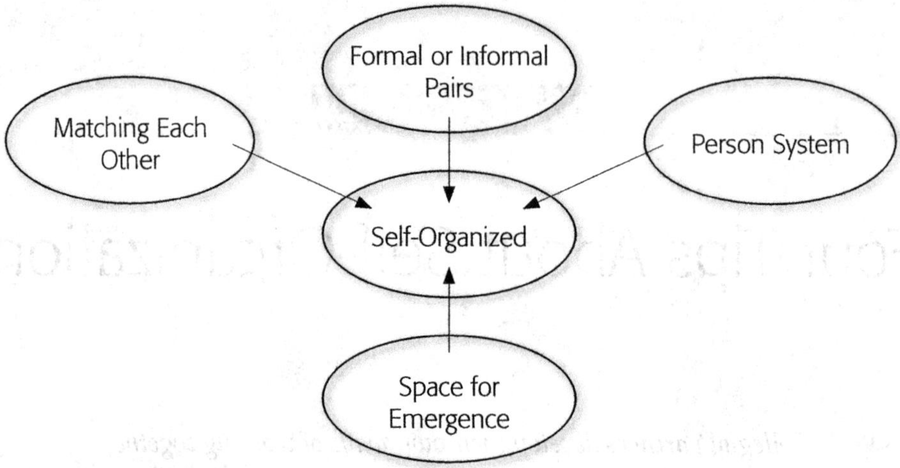

and differences in gender, age, and/or ethnic background. Other similarities and differences can be in religion, sexual preference, values, and/or class. The reasons someone might not match someone else are complex and may not be easy to determine; however, if there is significant mismatching, the relationship may not work well. I will provide additional information on similarities (redundancy) and differences (diversity) between mentors/coaches and novices/struggling teachers in Chapter 6.

Few Mismatches

Although the mentor coordinator at Lincoln carefully matched mentors and novices and the administration had hired coaches for major content areas, some teachers found others to help them. For instance, Mr. Cook appreciated his assigned mentor, but he had been Mrs. Herman's practice teacher, and even though she was also his content coach, Mr. Cook saw Mrs. Herman as his primary mentor. Mrs. Truitt said she agreed to become Mr. Nelson's informal mentor because he was not happy with his assigned one. For the most part the mentors, coaches, and teachers at Lincoln were happy with each other. Even so, most of them had other supportive relationships within the school, but none was quite like the mentor relationship.

> **Tip #1:** Program leaders might suggest mentor–novice pairs, but they might also allow individuals to choose other people with whom to work. Individuals need to advocate for themselves if there is a mismatch within a formal assignment. No one should be required to work with an assigned person. Program

leaders can help mentors and novices deal with potential mismatches by presenting the pairings as temporary. They might also encourage partners to evaluate their relationship at the end of the first few weeks of school and then to make a mutual decision about continuing to work together. School leaders can convey through their mentoring/coaching policies that it is not a failure on the part of either partner if the relationship does not work. School leaders might help novices or struggling teachers find alternative partners or encourage them to find their own new helpers. In Chapter 6, I present additional ideas about implementing temporary collegial partnerships as a "decentralized" process.

Formal and Informal Pairings

Relationships develop in a variety of ways, and it could be helpful to beginning teachers if school leaders match them with veterans at the beginning of the year. Leaders might allow the flexibility of choosing other helpful veterans as new teachers get to know their colleagues. Assigning collegial partners could be important initially because novices do not know which veterans might work best with them, and some could feel uncomfortable asking veterans to be their partners. Having both formally assigned mentors or coaches and informally chosen ones can add support and allow novices and struggling teachers the ability to experience helpful information from a variety of perspectives. For example, some novices who do not relate to their mentors as friends can still respect and implement their teaching suggestions; in time, they can find other veterans with whom they are able to develop friendships and with whom they feel a greater sense of support and caring. This variety provides both challenge and support, which can facilitate professional growth.

Collegial Partners and Friends

At Lincoln, teachers had both formally assigned and informally chosen mentors. A school leader assigned coaches, who were in some cases mentors and coaches at the same time, not just to individuals but also to teams. Mr. Hansen (novice) provided an excellent example of how help came to him both formally and informally. Mrs. Truitt, his mentor, provided help that obviously made a difference in how he developed as a teacher. However, he also highly valued Mr. Manzetti and his brother, who had introduced him to a *professional friends' network*. As a participant in the network, Mr. Hansen joined some of the younger teachers on Fridays after school to debrief and to enjoy each other's company away from the school. He also made some professional friends through his involvement in sports. For instance, Mr. Hansen coached basketball and his friends coached other sports. They showed their support for each other by attending each other's games. This informal support also played a tremendous role in Mr. Hansen's development as a teacher. He learned from his mentor that he could develop strategies to make him a more effective teacher, and he learned from his professional friends that he could develop and enjoy a teacher lifestyle.

> **Tip #2:** Invite and facilitate a variety of relationships among collegial partnerships. If administrators make sure that at least one person is providing support, they might leave it up to those seeking help to find their own professional friends. Administrators and other school leaders might also encourage or even facilitate socialization among teachers. Some ideas that can support team building and friend building include the following:
>
> - school leaders encourage teams to plan social events away from school at least once per quarter
> - grade level or content groups form sports teams that play each other
> - school leaders ask a group of teachers to form a hospitality committee, or teams take turns planning events for every major cultural celebration (e.g., Halloween, Thanksgiving, Christmas/Hanukkah/Kwanzaa, Valentine's Day, St. Patrick's Day, Easter/Passover)
> - peer groups invite those who are interested to socialize with them after school on Fridays

Space for Emergence

Most educators are familiar with *teachable moments*, those times when students are ready to learn what teachers are trying to teach. The complexity concept of *emergence* is similar to the teachable moment, except they differ in a significant way. Emergence captures complexity, whereas the teachable moment does not. In complexity, a teacher does not use a teachable moment to *cause* students to learn, even if they seem ready.

Emergence explains how the interaction between two people, regardless of their roles, can result in a change in both of them. The process is not one-way from teacher to learner; the process goes both ways between them.

For example, the novice or struggling teacher might say or do something that triggers a response from a partner, but the trigger from the novice or struggling teacher may have come as a response from something the partner said or did, which makes it difficult to determine where the learning started and where it ended. In other words, it was a complex interaction that is hard to trace from Point A to Point B. The process, in other words, is not linear.

Of all of the findings about mentoring and coaching, the concept of "space for emergence," is one of the most important (Kalin, Barney, & Irwin, 2010, p. 357). Some people might think of this space as where "teachable moments" occur or in the language of complexity, where co-created ideas might emerge. Mentors, coaches, and teachers might learn to create spaces that allow emergence to happen. Even though they cannot control what happens or emerges in those spaces, they can make those spaces more conducive to emergence, which I will explain in detail in Chapter 7.

My study examined how the concept of ecologically based sustainable capacity building helped to create this space (Mitchell & Sackney, 2009). (I will discuss Mitchell and Sackney's [2009] ideas in more detail in Chapter 7.) Similar ideas come from William Isaacs (1999), who called this kind of space for emergence a "container." Isaacs defined a container as a space that is safe for getting beyond politeness in order to resolve important and destructive conflicts (p. 239). In containers, mentors, coaches, and teachers either in dyads or groups might learn how to have productive dialogues based on their abilities to listen to each other, respect each other's perspectives, suspend their own perspectives in order to hear the perspectives of others, and develop the courage to voice their honest opinions. In the Activities section of this chapter, I provide directions for developing a "container." (I offer another strategy for developing a "container" in Chapter 7.)

Another excellent example of a space for emergence is the model proposed by Lave and Wenger (1991) called "communities of practice." In these communities, veterans help newcomers become members of the community through their support and guidance. Lave and Wenger suggested that twelve-step programs like Alcoholics Anonymous (AA) provide an example of a community of practice. In AA, people with similar concerns share the leadership within a program based on core principles and traditional structures. Veteran members welcome newcomers and act as sponsors for them if they ask. These kinds of programs have demonstrated both sustainability and good results for those who commit to them.

In the Trenches

Although in my study at Lincoln High School I did not directly observe collegial partnerships creating spaces for emergence, teachers and mentors told me stories about how they created them. When I talked to them in pairs, I could tell that they had been through a lot together and that they had found ways to resolve many school conflicts in the spaces they co-created. An excerpt from a story from Mrs. Herman sums up how mentors at Lincoln were willing to go into these spaces, which she metaphorically referred to as trenches:

> As a mentor, Mrs. Herman was willing to go "into the trenches" with her novices; however, she could not fight their battles for them. She could interpret, caution, share ideas, and care about them, but she could not fight their battles. With Mr. Cook, she was careful to ask him how he might handle a situation before explaining how she might deal with it. She armed the novices in her care with knowledge about the leadership; about the school culture, which included students, parents, and district personnel; and about resources that supported the curriculum. She backed them up as far as she could, but when it came to going into combat, which was possible in the administrative, school culture, and curriculum arenas, they had to advance, retreat, or leave the battlefield on their own. She also acknowledged that what might work for her as an older, veteran, and African-American woman may not work for a young, novice, and white male or female. In other words, she never assumed that she could provide a plan that any novices might universally apply. (Waterman, 2012, pp. 283–284)

From this excerpt, I understood that at Lincoln the "space for emergence" around conflict was like a trench in a war zone. The mentor, Mrs. Herman, used this space to help her mentees handle conflicts by providing critical insider information about the school culture, by providing a supportive stance towards mentees, and by engaging in complex conversations with them. In these conversations she asked her mentees critical questions that helped them discover their roles in the conflicts they were experiencing and how they might engage their existing skills or develop new ones to deal with those conflicts. As an example, when Mr. Cook was frustrated because his students would not listen to him, Mrs. Herman helped him discover that he needed to use his familiarity with pop culture to meet his students halfway between that culture and academic objectives. This method worked beautifully. Mr. Cook learned to connect with his students and they with him, greatly decreasing the conflict between teacher and students.

Tip #3: Administrators can provide time for mentors and coaches to meet with novices and struggling teachers in order to develop spaces for emergence. However, these spaces may not develop if teachers do not understand their importance and know how to create them. Administrators or other school leaders can facilitate the creation of these spaces if they value them and learn how to create them themselves. They might then show partners how these spaces might work by modeling them in faculty meetings. They can assure faculty that they do not want to gloss over the inevitable conflicts of working in a school system, and that their school is committed to providing safe places for professional sharing of ideas and dealing with challenges. At a faculty meeting, for example, school leaders might role-play a complex conversation that addresses a specific school conflict. Some example questions to guide the conversation could be as follows:

- ♦ What responsibility does each person have for the conflict around … ?
- ♦ What might each person do to change his or her response to the conflict?
- ♦ How might the conflict become an opportunity for growth?
- ♦ What would happen to … if we did not have this conflict?
- ♦ What can each person gain if we no longer have this conflict at our school?

The best way collegial partners can create space for emergence is to resist giving advice and instead demonstrate a sincere curiosity about how to co-create understanding, commitments, uses of skills and talents, and personal accountability. They can express this curiosity in respectful and authentic questions within complex conversations. When answering those questions, conversation participants should be honest about how they feel. They should do their best to focus on themselves and avoid personally attacking or criticizing other participants in the conversation.

Person System

Even though modern science has discovered a great deal about how human brains function and how they learn, what goes on in human minds or how people truly feel is complex and difficult to understand. For example, Jane may wake up feeling depressed and lonely, but when she walks into the school building, she may respond to certain people who ask how she is doing that she feels fine. However, when she sees her mentor or coach in the teachers' work room, she may confess that she is not feeling that great. We may know our own thoughts and feelings, but it is difficult for us to know how another person thinks and feels. In our society, we tend to believe that by analyzing the words and actions of others we can figure them out, but we can form lots of assumptions that could be wrong.

The reason it is so important to understand that we cannot actually read minds or know true feelings is that the situations in which people share their thoughts and feelings and the person or persons with whom they are sharing them play significant roles in what those expressions mean. With the person system, therefore, I am still thinking of a person in relation to others.

Since we can only make assumptions based on what individuals say and how they behave, our assumptions can sometimes be faulty. Mentors, coaches, and others do not have access to the minds, the feelings, and all of the other interactions that may have played a role in forming their charges' feelings and actions. If mentors, coaches, or their partners believe they are working with someone who has some personal deficiencies, this could create problems. Having a deficit perspective (Gold, 1996) when it comes to assessing the abilities of others can weaken or even destroy relationships.

Stay Out of the Office!

One of the best examples of personal differences between a mentor and a mentee is the relationship between Mr. Manzetti and Mrs. Baker. Mr. Manzetti was adamant that Mrs. Baker should resolve her own classroom discipline problems rather than involve administrators. But Mrs. Baker believed that she needed the office to handle many of her classroom concerns. She also believed that her fourth-period class was so challenging that she had no other option but to call for help. As a matter of fact, she often had at least one administrator and one security guard helping her on a regular basis. It seemed that the inability of Mr. Manzetti and Mrs. Baker to come to terms with their different perspectives may have played a role in their mentor–mentee relationship.

> **Tip #4:** Decision makers and practitioners who understand that personal differences can affect mentor/coach and novice/struggling teacher relationships might take steps to make sure they do what is necessary in order to better understand each other. By discouraging a deficit perspective (Gold, 1996) in favor of an appreciative perspective (e.g., Cooperrider,

Whitney, & Stavros, 2007), more creative solutions to conflict could emerge. If teachers and administrators make a personal commitment to having complex conversations, they will hold themselves accountable for establishing a positive, respectful, and caring school culture.

Semeniuk and Worrall (2000) suggested that one of the most beneficial aspects of their mentor–mentee relationship was that neither one of them ever questioned the other's competence. Although this could be difficult in some situations and with some people, it seems to be a worthy aspiration that could have many benefits.

Saving Time and Money

Schools can save time and money by recognizing that mentors/coaches and teachers find ways to work together that a central location or thorough and extensive training and coordination cannot control. School leaders might save time and money by not assigning someone to match and monitor how mentors, coaches, and teachers work together. By expecting and allowing teams to self-organize, school leaders might avoid the added and costly expense of matching and monitoring.

Mentors and coaches who do not have their own classrooms should consider helping in other teachers' classrooms, in order to qualify as peer helpers. According to Ladyshewsky (2006), when one person has more power than another, it is less likely that they will learn from each other. He also said that being viewed as an expert can unbalance the level of power between individuals. I believe that giving mentors and coaches special privileges, such as an office and the freedom to schedule their own time, can also unbalance the power. Classroom teachers might envy them and suspect them, rightly or not, of being aligned with administrators. From my personal experience, when I had my own office and the freedom to plan my own time, an administrator said to me, "Now you're one of *us*!" I learned that many of the veteran teachers wanted my job so that they could leave the classroom without becoming administrators. In sum, school leaders and collegial partners need to make sure to do their best to equalize power rather than unbalancing it. (I will talk about this more in Chapter 4. In that chapter I provide a chart comparing and contrasting full-time mentors and coaches with those who are classroom-based.)

Activities

The Team Compact

One way to welcome new teachers into an already functioning team (e.g., fifth-grade team, social-studies team) is to ask the team members to spend some time in an already scheduled meeting to draw up a "compact" that tells teachers new to the team what they can expect.

Step 1: Meet as a team to compose the compact. (See "The Team Compact Example.")

Step 2: Type it and print it on a formal-looking page (e.g., find an official looking border for the page). Create lines for members of the team to sign and leave a space or spaces for the new teacher or teachers to sign.

Step 3: In a team meeting read the compact aloud to the new member or members of the team.

Step 4: All sign the compact.

The Team Compact Example

Science Team Compact

We the members of the Science Department at Lincoln High School promise to do the following for our new teachers:

1. Keep our doors open and ourselves available to help in any way we can.
2. Suspend our judgment and criticism of you because we know how difficult the first year of teaching can be.
3. Promise to do our best to never to let you sink.
4. Respect you and value you as a new member of our team.
5. Do everything in our power to help you succeed at our school.

Signed:

____________________ Teacher

____________________ Teacher

____________________ Teacher

____________________ Teacher

____________________ New Teacher

Welcome Wagon

This activity can be a fun and friendly way to welcome new teachers to the team.

Step 1: Find a vehicle for the materials you will place on the "Welcome Wagon." It could be a projector cart or an actual wagon if someone has access to one of those.

Step 2: Decide as a team what you would like to put in the wagon. Some suggestions:

- ♦ food (e.g., candy, cookies, sodas, or healthy snacks)
- ♦ useful teacher supplies (e.g., erasers, staplers, hole punchers, markers)
- ♦ books (e.g., special first-year teacher survival books or helpful content materials)
- ♦ art supplies for making bulletin boards (e.g., construction paper, posters, borders)
- ♦ other survival materials (be creative!)

Step 3: At an appointed time before school starts and before the new teacher has started dealing with her room, one or more team members might agree to take the wagon by and welcome the new teacher.

Symbolic Gifts

This activity could facilitate a beginning of the kinds of conversations that help teachers build safe places for sharing honestly with each other. It could be used in a group or a process between mentor/coach and teacher.

Veteran teachers think of a meaningful gift or gifts for a new teacher or new teachers who will be joining their department or joining them in a mentoring or coaching relationship. Each gift can be symbolic of something important in the life of a teacher, and the giver should take time to explain what the gift represents and why he or she is giving it. Some suggestions:

- ♦ A picture of a serene scene. Example of an explanation: I am giving you this picture of a place I go to in my mind when I am feeling overwhelmed. I use this picture to help me relax. I am giving this picture to you with the hope that you will also find a place of serenity even when you are feeling overwhelmed.
- ♦ A picture of a clock or a real clock. Example of an explanation: I am giving you this clock to remind you that teaching takes a lot of your time, especially at first, but eventually you will learn to manage your time so that you will also have time for yourself and time to enjoy this wonderful profession.

- A picture of a ruler or a real ruler. Example of an explanation: I am giving you this ruler because I know how it feels to have your work constantly measured. We all have gifts and talents, and sometimes we feel that we are measured not by our strengths but by our weakness. I am giving you this ruler to remind you to keep measurement in perspective.
- A picture of a student. Example of an explanation: I am giving you a picture of one of my favorite students, who helped me learn that students do not care how much we know—until they know that we care for them.

Gift Cards

If you like to be creative, you might make a series of cards to give to new teachers in a group or between individuals. These cards can be invitational, such as one that welcomes teachers to "vent their frustrations." (See following example.) Teachers might also explain why they are providing the card, and they should commit to acknowledging the card when it is "redeemed" by the person to whom they gave it.

Venting Card

This card entitles its owner to 30 minutes of free Venting Time.

Redeem as Necessary!

From: ____________________

Example of an explanation: I am giving you this Venting Card because I know how important it can be to vent your frustrations. I promise to be a safe place for you to vent.

Other ideas for "gift cards" are as follows:

- Substitute Time: "I'll take your class during my planning period."
- Extra Duty Coverage: "I'll take your extra duty for you."
- Parent Help: "I'll help you think of a way to deal with an angry parent."
- Lesson Plan: "I'll share a favorite lesson plan with you."

Trust Building

Trust can be difficult to establish; however, it is essential that trust form the basis of helping relationships such as mentors–mentees. Trust-building activities are abundant and can help mentors, coaches, or group leaders who work with them to begin this process. The following outline describes several kinds of trust activities. Please note that one of the most critical aspects of these activities is the "debriefing" that follows them. Allow plenty of time to talk in detail about the effects of participating in the activity for all involved, including the leader. You may find some of these activities useful:

1. Activities using a blindfold or closing eyes (in pairs)
    - **Running Free:** One person leads the other from a slow walk to a fast run.
    - **Trust Lean:** One person catches the other person as he or she falls. (Note that the sizes of the participants is important in the pairing and that someone who agrees to fall might start small based on comfort levels.)
    - **Blind Crossing:** A seeing partner uses verbal directions to guide a blindfolded partner to him or her.
    - **Mine Field:** Scatter objects around a large room, such as a gymnasium. The seeing partner uses verbal directions to guide the blindfolded one through the area.
2. Activities using a blindfold or closing eyes (in groups)
    - **Willow in the Wind:** With eyes closed or blindfolded, one person in the middle of the group does a trust lean into the group and is moved around the circle by them.
    - **Blind Walk:** The leader facilitates the blindfolding of all members of the group and asks them to link themselves together by holding the hand of the person next to them and the shoulder of a person in front of them. The leader then takes the blindfolded, linked group on a walk. This walk can last from ten minutes to two hours depending on the level of challenge the leader is seeking.

3. Activities addressing eye contact
   - **Eye Contact and Eye Contact with Touch:** Partners stand facing each other at a comfortable distance for both of them. They maintain eye contact for sixty seconds. They may also choose to hold hands (or not).
   - **Proximity:** Pairs stand facing each other at a comfortable distance. They move a little closer and talk about how that feels, and then they move farther apart and say how that feels.
4. Activities for large groups

   Slice 'n' Dice: A large group forms a gauntlet by using their arms in a chopping motion. One at a time, members of the group run through the gauntlet.
5. Activities involving jumping
   - **Leap of Faith:** A person jumps from a platform that is not too high off the ground in order to grab a rope hanging nearby.
   - **Bungee Jumping:** A person attached to a bungee cord jumps from a considerable height (e.g., 100 m.).
   - **Base Jumping:** Using special equipment, a person jumps into space from a major height (e.g., 300 m.).[1]

Another excellent site provides directions for the following activities:

- The human knot
- 4 Up
- Make a team with …
- Listen to me!
- What are we talking about?
- Blindfolded assault course
- Something fishy's going on
- Drawing twins
- Bat and moth[2]

[1] Adapted from Wilderdom (2009).

[2] Adapted from "Diversity and Dialogue" (n.d.).

Creating a Container #1

Caution: Do not try this activity if the people involved feel that the relationships are unequal or that a member of the group is evaluating them.

Use this activity for pairs or in small groups. Participants can take turns answering these kinds of questions:

- We want to form a safe place to talk honestly and openly to each other. What is the best way for us to listen to each other (e.g., take turns, avoid interrupting)?
- How might we best show our respect for each other as we talk (e.g., avoid giving advice, criticizing, judging)?
- How might we show that we are keeping an open mind and suspending our own perspectives so that we truly hear perspectives other than our own (e.g., make a personal commitment to practicing open-mindedness and trying to live up to that commitment, admitting when we are not doing so and correcting our error)?
- How might we make sure we each voice our honest beliefs and feelings in a respectful manner (e.g., agree not to stay silent even if what we believe does not agree with someone else)?
- Given that we are fallible human beings who may breach the confidentiality and trust established in this group, how might we address mistakes members could potentially make that threaten the safety of our container (e.g., asking for forgiveness and forgiving)?
- How will we make sure we prioritize and sustain our container for as long as we need it (e.g., make personal commitments to making it a priority, have a fixed time and place that is honored by all)?

See Chapter 7, page 146, for another method for creating a "container."

Chapter 3

Nine Tips About Close Communication

Collegial partners closely communicate often and in many ways.

Short-Range Relationships

Complex systems such as schools and collegial partnerships are by their nature short-ranged. This means that although decisions made by more distant systems, like administrative teams and districts, are important; the distinct manner in which complex systems address those decisions occur between those who are most closely associated with each other.

According to Davis and Sumara (2006), complex systems exchange information through "short-range relationships" (p. 5). What this means in terms of complex systems is that parts of the system that are in close proximity (e.g., collegial partnerships) *cohere* (i.e., connect) more strongly or have stronger ties with each other than they have with other parts of the system that are more distant (e.g., school leaders, district decision makers). If we go back to the dancer metaphor I used in the Introduction, those dancers exemplify a short-range relationship similar to collegial partnerships. For example, human dancers are not only close, but they are also interdependent. These dancers constantly exchange information about their responses to the dance structure (e.g., a waltz) and the source of the music (e.g., a band director and band or a sound system), which are more distant or centralized systems. Even though the dancers respond to those more distant or centralized systems, they are not dependent on those systems to determine how they dance together so that their dance is their own. Alignment with the distant or centralized systems and with each other makes the dancers both "efficient and robust" (Davis & Sumara, 2006, p. 5). (Note that the concept of short-range relationships is important to understand in terms of decentralized systems, which I will explain in Chapter 6.)

Figure 3.1 shows how mentors/coaches and novices/struggling teachers (ST) have short-range relationships so that they constantly exchange information and co-depend on each other without being strongly dependent on school culture/leadership. Note that the interacting arrows between the mentor/coach and novice/ST are shorter, which shows that they can be more efficient in their implementation of ideas. The arrows between them and the school culture/leadership show that they still connect, but they are farther apart, which makes them robust. Robustness occurs when a weaker link or connection with the distant system (e.g., administrative teams and district decision makers) allows those who are in a short-range relationship (e.g., collegial partnership) to be creative and relevant as they implement ideas locally.

As I said in Chapter 3, collegial partners self-organize so that those who have the greatest opportunity to work together determine how they will respond to school policies and procedures. This feature of complex systems reminds us that although ideas from distant and centralized decision makers are highly important, no matter how well-intentioned or well-conceived they may be, they have weaker influence over implementation than those who are closest to each other. School leaders and teachers can view this feature of

Figure 3.1 Short-Range Relationships

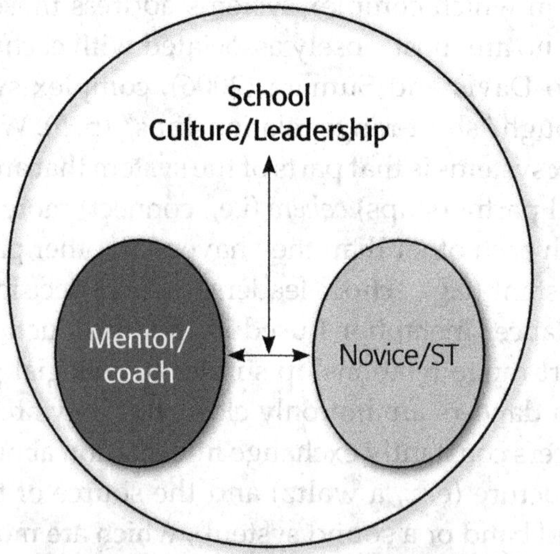

Source: Reproduced from Waterman (2012, p. 259).

Figure 3.2 Close Communication

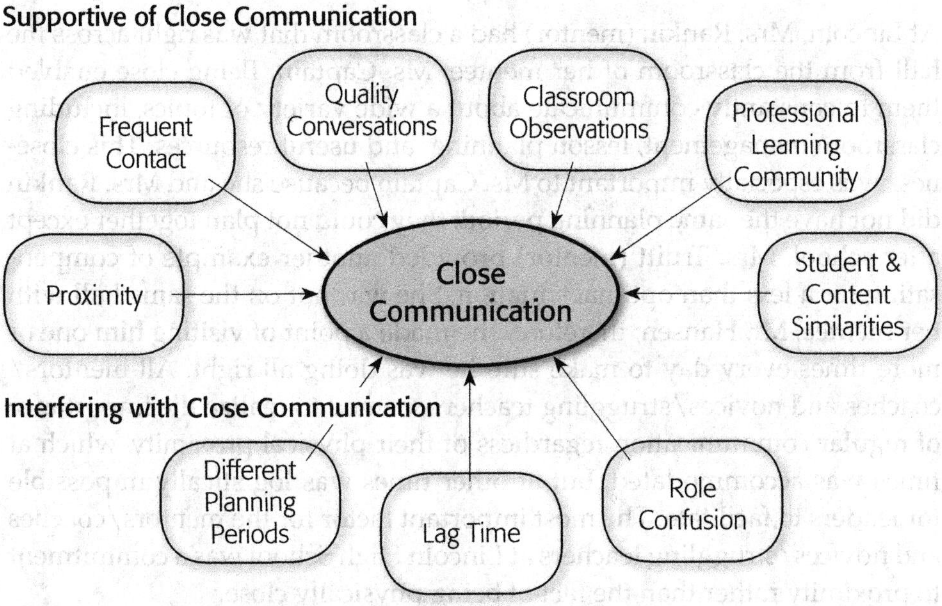

complex systems as positive if they recognize and respect the importance of *both* distant and short-range relationships. I found a great deal of evidence at Lincoln that demonstrated the positive aspects of close communications within partnerships and their responses to centralized decisions. In Figure 3.2, I show that some school structures were supportive of close communication, with elements such as proximity, frequent contact, quality conversations, classroom observations, professional learning community, and student and content similarities. Elements interfering with communication were different planning periods, lag time, and role confusion.

Supportive of Close Communication

Proximity

It seems optimal for collegial partners to have classrooms and/or offices near each other. It is important for teachers to be able to step next door or down the hall to communicate with their partners; on the other hand, those teachers and their partners who are not on the same floor or hallway might take time to visit more often to compensate for the distance. Close physical proximity makes getting together more convenient and can play a role in the development and sustainability of partnerships; however, it is not essential. When school leaders cannot provide this proximity, committed staff can compensate by increasing their visits to those they want to help.

Right Across the Hall

At Lincoln, Mrs. Rankin (mentor) had a classroom that was right across the hall from the classroom of her mentee, Ms. Captain. Being close enabled them to constantly communicate about a wide variety of topics, including classroom management, lesson planning, and useful resources. This closeness was especially important to Ms. Captain because she and Mrs. Rankin did not have the same planning period; they could not plan together except after school. Mrs. Truitt (mentor) provided another example of compensating for a less than optimal situation. She was not on the same hall with her mentee, Mr. Hansen; therefore, she made a point of visiting him one or more times every day to make sure he was doing all right. All mentors/coaches and novices/struggling teachers seemed to realize the importance of regular communication regardless of their physical proximity, which at times was accommodated, but at other times was logistically impossible for leaders to facilitate. The most important factor for the mentors/coaches and novices/struggling teachers at Lincoln High School was a commitment to proximity rather than the fact of being physically close.

> **Tip #1:** School leaders should consider making efforts to place collegial partners near each other. If this is not possible, partners can make a commitment to proximity in their relationships, regardless of their actual location. They might consider keeping a Connections Journal or Log, which is suggested in the Activities section of this chapter. By making a point of recording evidence of connections, partners can assess their commitment to closeness regardless of proximity.

Frequent Contact

Talking to each other in person or via email on a daily basis is extremely important for helping relationships. Even brief conversations can help develop problem-solving relationships. Even if mentors and coaches do not communicate with their charges daily, it is important to know that the option for daily communication is available.

Part-Time Collegial Partners

Most of the teacher helpers at Lincoln said that they talked to the person they were helping on a daily basis. An exception was Mrs. Stanley (mentor/coach), who was only in the building two days per week. It was interesting that even though Mrs. Stanley and Mrs. Lawson, her mentee, had the capability of making contact on a daily basis through email or by cell phone, they did not. Mrs. Stanley's dual roles as mentor and coach further limited her ability to contact Mrs. Lawson frequently.

Tip #2: As with proximity, commitment to frequency of contact can be more important than easy access to each other. It is a good idea to eliminate as many barriers as possible to increase the likelihood of daily communication between partners. Decision makers and collegial partners may consider having complex conversations about the barriers to closeness they experience in their relationships. During these conversations, they can identify some barriers to closeness and then creatively determine some "barrier busters" that could facilitate more closeness in their relationships. Probably the best barrier buster would be having the same planning period, but if that is not possible, collaborative thinking might have the result of discovering other barrier busters, such as the following:

- Teams and/or departments could take turns having breakfast or lunch together while others cover their duties. For example, the Social Studies department could get together on Mondays, Math on Tuesdays, English on Wednesdays, Science on Thursdays, and support staff on Fridays. Electives could also be on a schedule such as Arts on Mondays, Languages on Tuesdays, Technologies on Wednesdays, Physical Education on Thursdays, and other electives on Fridays.
- Teachers and administrators might cover for collegial partners during testing or silent reading times so they might get together.
- Partners might sign up to do activities together such as performing school duties together, co-coaching teams or club sports, or cosponsoring an after-school club.

Quality Conversations

Collegial partners must meet every day to communicate with each other, and their communication must also have quality. In most studies, including mine, it is difficult to assess the quality of conversations that participants report rather than those that researchers observe. It is especially difficult to assess quality based on survey reports that quantify it. One of my participants, Mrs. Truitt (mentor), suggested that the best way to determine if mentors and coaches were having quality interactions with the teachers they were helping was to note the *results* of those interactions.

Mrs. Truitt's Suggestion

In an excerpt from a story drawn from Mrs. Truitt's interview, she provided an interesting suggestion for qualifying collegial partnership interactions:

> Mrs. Truitt replied that the "number of contact hours were not important" as long as the mentees felt like they had "someone to go to when a problem" occurred, and they had "somebody" they could "trust." To Mrs. Truitt that was the "big issue with the mentor." It was not that she sat down with her mentee "for an hour every other Thursday." It was the fact that her mentee knew that if he needed anything, he knew he could "absolutely come to" her. The mentee could sit and talk to the mentor "for four hours and not make a difference, but if he [had] a problem" and the mentor went up to administration and addressed it, that was "more powerful." (Waterman, 2012, p. 267)

Tip #3: Decision makers and collegial partners may find ways to judge the quality of their interactions by noticing the outcomes of those interactions rather than counting the number of times they get together. They may have complex conversations during which they establish the value of reflecting with each other about the quality of their interactions. I do not recommend more paperwork so that collegial partners have to fill out reports that rate the quality of their conversations; however, decision makers may create time to have conversations with them to talk about their relationships and what they have accomplished by working together. By making the time and expressing interest in the quality and progress of the relationships rather than creating more paperwork accountability, decision makers may find out valuable information. If decision makers ignore the relationships or insist on getting information about the relationships through paperwork, they could lose valuable information about the school culture and their faculty's needs.

Classroom Observations

Learning from observing or co-teaching seems to deepen the level of communication available to collegial partners. For instance, seeing someone model a strategy is far more useful than merely hearing about it or practicing it in simulated activities in professional training sessions. Mentors and coaches, who do not have regular classroom duties, are more likely to be able to model lessons for novices and struggling teachers, and it is difficult for teachers to observe those who have their same planning period. Some teachers who work with pre-service teachers in a practice teaching situation have excellent opportunities to watch how someone with more experience handles classroom management with challenging students; however, practice teachers, who come into schools having recently taken courses in content or pedagogy, often have useful skills to demonstrate to the cooperating teachers with whom they are assigned. The word *observation* intimidates some teachers, perhaps because they associate it with evaluation of their job performance. Some teachers might be less committed to the processes of observing one another because of the negative connotation the word *observation* carries.

Observations at Lincoln

At Lincoln, all of the collegial partners teach their classes, but only a few of the novices had seen partners teach their own classes. The best use of observation seemed to come from cooperating teacher–pre-service teacher relationships. For example, Mrs. Rankin and her mentee, Ms. Captain, taught closely together when Ms. Captain was Mrs. Rankin's practice teacher, and the result was that they formed a partnership based on mutual respect and idea sharing. Mrs. Herman and Mr. Cook, who were also in a practice teacher–cooperating teacher relationship, learned a great deal from observing each other. For example, Mrs. Herman admired the way Mr. Cook took her ideas and put his own twist on them. She admired Mr. Cook's creativity and his ability to connect with students. Mr. Cook credited Mrs. Herman with helping him move past his initial shock regarding the behavior of the student population at Lincoln so that he was able to survive his first semester.

> **Tip #4:** School leaders may have a positive effect on a culture of helping if they promote the practice of teachers observing each other. It is highly important that school leaders convey a strong message to all members of the faculty that collegial partners' observations are completely separate from evaluations. Having the observations go both ways between partners is important because it conveys the message that both are willing to make their practices transparent. The more the process becomes routine and the more participants experience positive rather than negative responses to opening themselves up for feedback, the better the process will work to create a culture of helping. School leaders and collegial partners might use a group method such

as "Lesson Study" to provide structure for teacher-to-teacher observations or they might develop their own procedures for observing each other (Richardson, 2004). They should include such information as what they will observe (e.g., certain parts of the class, the whole class) and how they will talk about that observation (e.g., constructive feedback only, non-judgmental). If the observations go both ways, it seems more likely that all participants will develop methods for providing caring and constructive—rather than judgmental—feedback.

Professional Learning Communities

The structure of learning communities can facilitate the development and sustainability of close relationships; however, they do not guarantee them. In Chapter 1, I explained that professional communities can provide a supportive context for collegial partnerships; on the other hand, because a structure is only as facilitative as the people who participate in it allow it to be, those who are in close relationships in learning communities determine its success or failure. In learning communities, members share leadership and no one person has the authority to control the group. Unfortunately, this is not always the case. Some participants in learning communities do not understand their own power to create a workable space, and they let those to whom they abdicate power control the learning community space. In some cases, members of the community may inadvertently or strategically convey that they have greater power to control the community by virtue of their roles or experiences. In the case of novices who may not feel entitled to equal power to influence the group, it could be up to veterans to welcome their participation and to help them feel empowered. In addition, administrative teams can have a tremendous effect on the functioning of learning communities. They might lend their support to one or more members of the learning community (such as mentors and coaches), thus giving certain members power over others. In this situation, trust is affected, making safe and shared leadership unlikely to occur.

The most useful professional communities share power equally and provide opportunities for collegial partnerships to do some of the following:

- create joint lesson plans and assessments
- resolve classroom management issues
- share important policy and content or grade level information
- build supportive and caring relationships

Lincoln's Learning Communities

At Lincoln High School, some of the teachers thrived on their involvement with their learning community. For example, Mrs. Herman (mentor/coach) helped one of her content-aligned teams save considerable time and effort by collaborating within a learning community to develop a single lesson plan that they each implemented. By writing a single lesson plan, they not only saved some time and effort for individual members of the team but also were better able to align how they taught shared objectives. This learning community provided content alignment as well as a kind of unity that addressed student behavior issues.

The learning community worked well for Mrs. Herman's content-aligned team, but not for everyone at Lincoln. Some of my participants said their learning community meetings became gripe sessions and wasted their precious time. Although school leaders at Lincoln required learning communities and created time in teachers' schedules for them to meet, the success or failure of a learning community hinged on a complex set of circumstances rather than easily identifiable factors.

> **Tip #5:** Learning communities can be highly useful for collegial partnerships; however, school leaders may need to demonstrate clearly that they value these types of communities, and they may need to model what it means to work together in this capacity. Those involved in a learning community may want to use the activities "Professional Learning Community: Our Space" (page 70) and "How We Work Together at Our School" (page 73) to help them share responsibility for their learning community. Some other ideas for keeping the community on track include taking turns leading the meeting, sharing the responsibility for creating an agenda, rotating the responsibility of taking notes at the meeting, and making sure everyone agrees on norms such as when, where, and how often to meet, and what kinds of events might excuse someone from attending.

Student and Content Similarities

When teachers teach similar content and have similar students, they have the potential to become close. Closeness allows them to share ideas about classroom management and pedagogy. They can co-plan lessons and formative assessments in order to decrease individual work load and increase alignment of learning opportunities for students. Alignment might be lateral, as in grade similarity, or it can be vertical, as in teachers working together to make sure students are prepared for moving forward in course difficulty. Having similar students and content areas makes it much easier to apply the benefits of collaboration.

Lincoln Example

At Lincoln, the majority of mentors, coaches, and teachers were closely aligned based on subjects and students they taught. In one example, Mrs. Truitt (mentor) did not teach the same grade level as her mentee Mr. Hansen, but Mr. Hansen was teaching the lower grade students who would eventually, if they were successful, become Mrs. Truitt's students in the upper grade. In being vertically aligned, Mrs. Truitt was able to let Mr. Hansen know what his students needed to learn and be able to do to be successful in her class. Mr. Hansen was able to then tell his students that he had heard directly from Mrs. Truitt what they should be focusing on in preparation for the upper-level course. Having vertical alignment served to bring Mrs. Truitt and Mr. Hansen closer together than they had been when the subjects they taught and the students they taught were developmentally different. Another example of closeness occurred among the teachers who taught the same program. For example, one of my participants, two other teachers at her grade level, and her mentor/coach learned to teach the same program. This small group of teachers, in collaboration with Mrs. Herman, their mentor/coach, wrote joint lesson plans and provided constant support to one another.

> **Tip #6:** If possible, match mentors and coaches with novices and struggling teachers who teach the same subjects and students at the same developmental level. If that is not possible, novices and struggling teachers might ask for help from those other than their collegial partners who share similar subjects and students. School leaders might encourage novices and struggling teachers to seek these relationships, and they may also provide ideas for them about to whom they might make a request for help. Within a culture of helping, the process of asking and accepting help from those other than formally assigned mentors/coaches but who align best in terms of teaching assignments could be seamless and simple.

Interfering with Close Communication

In most schools, it is simply not feasible to ensure that all collegial partnerships have the luxury of a structure that completely facilitates the possibility for easily getting together on a regular basis. However, there are some dilemmas that can have an especially negative effect on closeness. I will mention three: different planning periods, lag time, and role confusion.

Different Planning Periods

When classroom-based mentors and coaches have planning periods that differ from their partners, it seems less likely that they will be able to help with planning. Most teachers accept that they have to stay after school for faculty meetings, parent-teacher conferences, coaching assignments, and other administratively determined meetings, but they count on being able to leave school otherwise. They believe that their planning period is "their" time, and that it should be protected for planning purposes. Therefore, it is difficult for mentors and coaches to expect to plan, *on a regular basis*, with their partners after school.

The Only One with Third-Block Planning

Ms. Captain (novice) was a great sport about the fact that in her department, she was the only one with third-block planning. When the rest of her team got together, she was teaching, and when she had planning, she often wandered up to the teachers' lounge for company. Even though a coach helped teachers in her department, she recalled very few occasions when they got together during her planning period. Her coach, Mrs. Stanley, was only in the building two days per week. Fortunately, Ms. Captain was resourceful, and she found ways to compensate for being alone during third block.

> **Tip #7:** If at all possible, collegial partners should have the same planning period, but if that is not possible, school leaders may help them find other times to meet together. It is important that school leaders acknowledge that the situation is not optimal and that they appreciate the partners by compensating them for a less than optimal situation. For example, school leaders could allow those mentors/coaches who do not have the same

planning periods with their novices/struggling teachers to "get a pass" on covering school events and duties that other faculty members share. Or members of their team or department might step in to cover class time in order to allow them time to meet during the school day.

Lag Time

Most people would agree that getting off to a good start at the beginning of the year is crucial. Unfortunately, extenuating factors can sometimes make it impossible for collegial partners to get together at the very beginning of the school year. It is natural that novices would feel left to their own devices if there were lag time in their connection with a partner. If it is not possible at the very beginning of the year to match a novice or struggling teacher with a partner, it is important for teams or administrators to provide that support.

Mrs. Lawson's Lag Time Dilemma

When Mrs. Lawson began teaching at Lincoln, the mentor coordinator had not been able to find a qualified mentor/coach to meet her needs. Mrs. Lawson went for about a month before the mentor coordinator drafted Mrs. Stanley to help her. Mrs. Stanley, who came out of retirement to function as a part-time mentor/coach, was also the coach for Mrs. Lawson's entire department, and she was only in the building, as previously mentioned, two days per week. During the time before Mrs. Lawson had a formally assigned mentor, she sought help from a teacher who had a year's more experience than she. Mrs. Lawson was able to compensate for the lag time she experienced in having a formally assigned mentor at the beginning of the year.

Tip #8: School leaders should make every effort to provide novices and struggling teachers with someone to help them from the very beginning of school and especially before the students arrive. If these leaders are unable to find a formal partner for a novice or struggling teacher at the very beginning of the school year, departments or grade level teams might temporarily share the partnership responsibility, or one member of the department or grade level team might agree to be a temporary partner until a school leader can find a permanent one. The first step toward finding a solution to this challenge is making a commitment to make sure all novices and struggling teachers have someone to help them from the very beginning of the year. In a culture of helping, school leaders and faculty should ensure that they never leave any of their teachers to their own devices.

Role Confusion

Given the complex nature of schools, it is often necessary that teachers and administrators play dual or even multiple roles within their schools. Most people seem to attribute more power to the roles of administrators or mentors and coaches than to novices or struggling teachers; however, some people in these roles recognize that it is only by sharing power that they can meet mutually established goals. For example, some people seem to be able to separate the authority that may accompany their roles from their ability to develop respectful and mutually satisfying relationships with others. Unfortunately some people use their roles to gain power over those whose roles seem less powerful. When this is the case, dual or multiple roles can generate problems especially for those who are functioning as mentor-coaches.

Acting as Equals

At Lincoln I saw an example of a mentor/coach who was able to integrate her dual roles with great success. She was able to do this because she did not use her role to gain power over others. She regularly made it clear that she saw herself as equal with her colleagues and that collaboration was more important to her than personal recognition or power. According to several participants in my study, it was well known throughout the school that she was a team player. On the other hand, I also heard about mentors and coaches who experienced some role confusion, thus damaging the trust they needed to establish in order to work with the novices and struggling teachers.

Tip #9: School leaders might avoid confusion and negative outcomes by clarifying roles and establishing a culture of helping based on mutuality rather than relationships of unequal power. The most problematic role confusion occurs when it is uncertain whether collegial partners align with novices or struggling teachers or with administrators. It is critically important that mentors and coaches build trust with novices and struggling teachers. If at any point someone does not feel a sense of trust within those helping relationships, the relationship is no longer useful. Within a culture of helping, school leaders and partnerships can address any breakdowns in trust that occur and can have complex conversations about how to resolve them. They might use an activity like the "Trust Meter" to focus on this important aspect of partnerships.

Saving Time and Money

Acknowledging the power of close connections among the teaching staff and their ability to coach each other toward useful teaching practices, school decision makers can avoid spending money on additional specialists or expensive consultants and trainers. Unfortunately, collegial partners must balance closeness with differences, as I will discuss in Chapter 6; therefore, school leaders might encourage and facilitate the introduction of new ideas that might emerge in the realm of useful teaching practices. The introduction of new ideas might come through in-house study groups or from presentations at faculty meetings. By making the assumption that healthy communities of practice will bring new members into the profession in a natural way and that many teachers are constantly looking for new ideas, teachers make best use of their time and do not waste it in training sessions.

Activities

Are We Close?

Mentors and coaches may choose to complete this activity together. They may do this in an individual session or in a group.

Step 1: Look at the questions on this handout.

Step 2: Take turns answering them by circling the dots under "yes" or "no" for your side of the handout. Then connect the dots, beginning with question 1 and drawing a line to each subsequent circled dot in numerical order. Notice if your answers are similar to or different from those of your partner.

Step 3: Based on the diagram, answer the bottom-line question: Are we close? Talk about what you find means to you in terms of working together.

Are We Close?				
	Teacher		Mentor/ Coach	
Question	No	Yes	Yes	No
1. Do we teach the same content?	▪	▪	▪	▪
2. Do we teach the same kinds of students?	▪	▪	▪	▪
3. Do we teach the same grade level?	▪	▪	▪	▪
4. Are our classrooms near each other?	▪	▪	▪	▪
5. Do we have the same level of technology skills?	▪	▪	▪	▪
6. Are we the same gender?	▪	▪	▪	▪
7. Are we the same race?	▪	▪	▪	▪
8. Are we approximately the same age?	▪	▪	▪	▪
9. Do we have the same marital status?	▪	▪	▪	▪
10. Are we from the same socioeconomic class?	▪	▪	▪	▪
11. Are we from the same town?	▪	▪	▪	▪
12. Are we from the same region of the country?	▪	▪	▪	▪
13. Are our family backgrounds similar?	▪	▪	▪	▪
14. Do we come from the same religious tradition?	▪	▪	▪	▪
15. Do we have similar recreational activities?	▪	▪	▪	▪
16. Do we share the same philosophy of learning?	▪	▪	▪	▪
17. Are our personalities similar (e.g., extrovert/ introvert, quiet/talkative)?	▪	▪	▪	▪
18. Do we have similar physical characteristics?	▪	▪	▪	▪
19. Did we major in the same thing in college?	▪	▪	▪	▪
20. Did we have similar experiences in high school?	▪	▪	▪	▪

People tend to think they are more alike than they really are. This diagram can present an interesting conversation-starter about the role closeness might play in the way two people work together and help each other.

Connection Journal or Log

Suggest that collegial partnerships keep a Connection Journal or Log that reflects specific occasions when they feel a connection. If teachers are already keeping a journal for general purposes, this topic might be added as a sub-category for special attention. At the end of the week or another designated time, mentors/coaches and teachers might share with each other the contents of their journals or logs, or they might choose one specific occasion from their journals or logs to present to each other. A Connection Log might look like this:

Connection Log

Name: ______________________________

Date	Time	How did we connect?	How I felt about it
2/7/12	4th Block	When you listened to me tell about how one of my students would not sit in his desk and I could not teach	I felt a sense of relief that I could vent my frustrations with you instead of taking them home with me.
2/9/12	1st Block	When I saw your smiling face at my door and knew if I needed your help, I could wave you in	Supported and cared for
2/9/12	4th Block	When we were talking about teaching that story and you told me that if I didn't like it I could find another one I like better	Pleased and relieved that you gave me permission to choose another story

Professional Learning Community: Our Space

With the possibility of confusion regarding community members' differing roles and levels of experience, it can be difficult to forget that, generally, the purpose of a professional community is to create a safe *co-owned* space for collaborative problem solving in which everyone accepts equal power and equal responsibility. Optimally, all members of the professional community feel equally empowered to respectfully share their perspectives, and community members make decisions collaboratively. None of the members of the group, by virtue of their roles and/or levels of experience, exercise more power or less power than other members.

In order to begin each group session, community members might consider asking and answering a set of questions or developing a purpose statement. The group might also consider revisiting these questions or purpose statement each time they meet in order to remind them to stay focused on their co-ownership of the community space. All community members are invited to accept their responsibility for the maintenance of the group purpose and to share responsibility for addressing that purpose. Please answer these questions for yourself, and then if you feel comfortable, share your answers with the group.

- Do you believe you have equal power and responsibility within this community? If not, why not?
- Do you feel safe to honestly share your perspectives? If not, why not?
- Are you content with the manner in which this professional community is functioning? If not, why not?

Eye Contact: Closeness Exercise

I mentioned this kind of activity in the Chapter 2; however, I would like to reiterate its usefulness here. Collegial partnerships or groups might benefit from participating in this experiment about comfort with closeness:

Step 1: Pairs of participants stand apart and then move toward each other until one or both of them decide to stop.

Step 2: These pairs stand as they are and take turns talking about how they decided when to stop moving closer to each other. This conversation will help participants become aware of their personal space needs and will facilitate an exploration about personal boundaries and comfort levels.

Step 3: Participants time themselves to see how long they can maintain eye contact without having to look away. They might discuss how long they maintained eye contact and notice who needed to look away first. Again, this facilitates conversation about personal space and boundaries.

Important: Caution participants that this is not a staring contest and that the one who looks away is not deficient in his or her ability to be close. It can help participants understand that eye contact is highly important to demonstrate connection within the complex realm of personal communication. For example, getting "eye to eye" with those to whom you are talking shows you care about what you are saying and that you care about what they are saying.

Matching Stories

Teachers are great storytellers, and this activity capitalizes on that natural skill. This activity is useful between mentors/coaches and novices/struggling teachers by themselves or in a larger group in which they pair off.

Step 1: Collegial partners have pads of paper on which to write, and they sit facing each other.

Step 2: Ask them to take turns telling the story of why they became a teacher. Give them a time limit of five minutes and tell those who are listening to take some notes about what they are hearing.

Step 3: After partners have shared and taken notes, ask them to identify commonalities among their stories.

Step 4: Ask partners to collaborate in order to construct a futuristic story about how the teacher who is new or struggling will become the teacher he or she is hoping to become. At this step participants acknowledge the intersection of idealism that brought them to teaching and the reality they faced when they actually joined a faculty. Participants can be encouraged to use fantasy that engages symbolism and metaphorical imagery (e.g., the new teacher becomes a hero who slays the dragons that represent school bullies or his or her own fears).

Step 5: If you are in a group setting, ask volunteers to share their stories and/or their responses to the process. It might also be enjoyable to act out these stories.

Connection Through Collage: I Becomes Us

Collegial partners can do this activity by themselves or in a group. In order to do this, participants will need markers, magazines, glue, scissors, any other desired art-making materials, and a piece of poster board.

Teacher	Us	Mentor/Coach

Step 1: Collegial partners get into pairs.

Step 2: They fold their poster board into a trifold and label it as shown in the example above.

Step 3: Concurrently, partners make collages that represent them as individuals.

Step 4: Individuals study the collages made by their partners. They have complex conversations about what they have observed, and they might ask questions about their partners' work.

Step 5: They identify common connections and create a new collage that represents "Us."

Step 6: Volunteers might share their work in a larger group, and they might display the collages in the school.

How We Work Together at Our School

This activity can promote complex conversations about how teachers at the school work together. It is useful for a specific team or for a whole faculty divided into smaller groups based on teams, grade levels, or departments. Materials needed for this activity are a flip chart for each group and a marker. Here are the steps:

Step 1: A volunteer or chosen leader invites members of the group to share stories about a time when they felt successful working together.

Step 2: After volunteers have shared their stories, someone agrees to take notes for the group and prepares to collect the answers to this question: What do these stories tell us about how we worked together at our school? Some possible answers might be:

- We talked about the ideas we had for teaching certain curriculum objectives.
- We helped each other with student discipline.
- We called parents as a team.

Step 3: Finally, someone agrees to collect the answers to this question: How do we plan to work together this school year? Some possible answers:

- We will share curriculum ideas at least once per week in our PLC.
- We will help each other find solutions to discipline problems.
- We will call parents as a team once a week.

Step 4: Someone agrees to type the list and send it to everyone on the team. They also may want to share their list with administrators. They may revisit the list at the end of each semester in order to adjust it or make additions.

Trust Meter

Collegial partners can periodically use this activity to determine where they stand on trust issues. They can do this anonymously if they choose. For example, instead of putting their name on the line, they could put whether they are a mentor, coach, novice, or struggling teacher. For each statement, respondents describe how comfortable they are saying certain things to the person or persons with whom they are working.

Trust Meter						
Directions: Circle the number that best represents your feelings.						
Name (Optional): ______________________ Date: ____________						
1. I can say how I feel about my students, colleagues, administrators, and the district.						
Low Trust						High Trust
1	2	3	4	5	6	7
2. I can say how I feel about our relationship.						
Low Trust						High Trust
1	2	3	4	5	6	7
3. I can say how I feel about my weaknesses (e.g., what I need to improve).						
Low Trust						High Trust
1	2	3	4	5	6	7
4. I can say how I feel about gaps in my content knowledge (e.g., what I need to learn).						
Low Trust						High Trust
1	2	3	4	5	6	7
5. I can say how I feel about my frustrations with my teaching practices.						
Low Trust						High Trust
1	2	3	4	5	6	7
6. I can say how I feel about ____________ (other).						
Low Trust						High Trust
1	2	3	4	5	6	7
Add up the numbers and get a total score. Obviously if the score is high, the trust is high and if the score is low, the trust is low.						
Total Score: __________						

After completing this activity, collegial partners should have a professional dialogue about the findings and they should decide what they might do to improve trust in their relationships.

Chapter 4

Three Tips About Identity

Many factors shape the identities of mentors and coaches, including the school context, those who implement mentor and coach roles, and how they serve novices and struggling teachers through those roles.

Closed Relationships Create Identity

Complex systems, such as collegial partnerships, are both structurally open and closed at the same time. They are open in ways that I will explain in Chapter 5. They are closed in that they remain stable as a specific relationship even though they are constantly exchanging matter and energy from outside the boundaries of that relationship. These "organizationally closed" systems thus have identities that describe them and distinguish them from other systems (Davis & Sumara, 2006, p. 5). The relationship between the mentor or coach and the novice or struggling teacher is a dyad, a two-person complex system whose identity differs from other types of helping relationships and which I call "collegial partnership." Using the dancing couple example, the two participants maintain their identity as a dancing couple only if they continue to dance together; otherwise, they are just two people. Just like the dancing couple, collegial partnerships determine their identity by what they do together. And if they stop doing those things, they are no longer identified as a partnership.

Figure 4.1 Mentor and Coach Identity

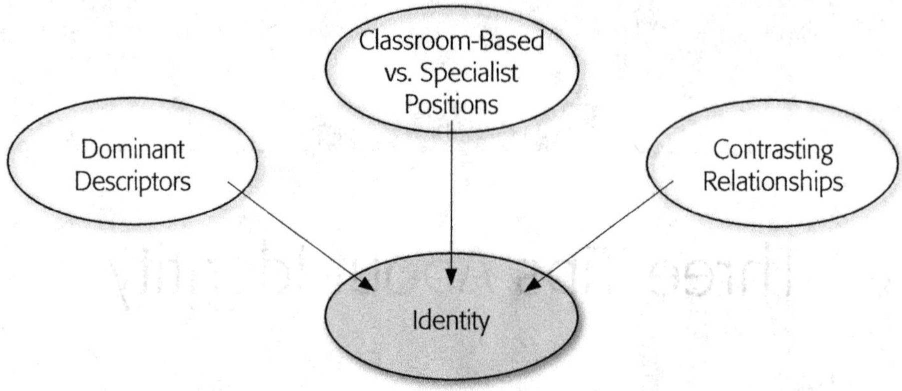

Mentor Identity

Another important aspect of the identity of a complex system is that it is similar to other mentor or coach designations, but at the same time it is unique. The similar nature of the identity of the mentor or coach is in the common use of the titles *mentor* and *coach*. The unique aspects of mentor and coach identities are based on where these roles occur, how the people in the roles implement them, and how those who receive mentoring and coaching interact with them. For example, the identity of mentors at Lincoln may differ considerably from the identity of mentors and coaches in other schools. In order to best explain mentor and coach identities, I will address three major areas: dominant descriptors, classroom-based versus full-time positions, and contrasting relationships. (See Figure 4.1.)

Dominant Descriptors

Recognizing the unique manner in which different school cultures identify mentoring and coaching roles, I caution readers to continually remind themselves that I am explaining what I found from conducting my study and from reading the literature on mentoring and coaching. My conclusions were also influenced by my personal experience of mentoring and coaching. Therefore, when I talk about my findings or ideas, I am not claiming that my explanations describe the identities of mentors and coaches in every setting, nor do I claim that my explanations of their identities represent the best or most useful practices for every setting. I encourage readers to use the ideas that are applicable and useful for them, but to disregard those ideas that are not.

Dominant Descriptors of Mentors at Lincoln

In order to capture a consensus description of the mentors at Lincoln High School, I gathered key phrases and inferred ideas from the stories my participants told me in their individual and mentor–novice interviews. I grouped some of the ideas that seemed to represent the same descriptors, and then I counted how often my participants used those descriptors when they talked about their experiences with mentoring. This is the list I generated from this process:

1. The mentors' knowledge of the school culture was superior to novices' knowledge of it.
2. The mentors had experience as teachers of challenging students that was superior to that of novices.
3. Mentors were respected, empowered, and trusted by school leadership but they aligned with novices.
4. Mentors and novices admired each other's practices.
5. Mentoring was a one-on-one commitment.
6. The mentors and novices had daily contact.
7. Mentor-novice dyads collaborated and shared ideas and materials.
8. Mentors could not stop administrators from dismissing novices.

Source: Waterman, 2012, pp. 104–105

Tip #1: School leaders and teachers should make sure they understand how all members of the faculty define the identities of mentors and coaches at their school. In some cases there will be consensus and in others there may be some disagreement about mentoring and coaching roles. If there are differences, school leaders might make every effort to help mentors or coaches and novices or struggling teachers clarify these roles and eliminate differences by having complex conversations with them. Some of the questions those who participate in these conversations might explore to clarify their relationships are

- What are you planning to gain from your relationship?
- How do you see yourself sharing your skills and abilities with each other?
- What are some stories about your relationship so far?
- How will you show your level of commitment and accountability within this relationship?

- ♦ How will you let the other person in the relationship know if you begin feeling confused, misunderstood, or uncomfortable with any aspect of the relationship?

School leaders and collegial partnerships might also use some of the activities at the end of this chapter to help them clarify their personal and relationship identities.

Classroom-Based vs. Full-Time Positions

A review of the recent research regarding the effect of mentoring on teacher retention (Waterman & He, 2011) concluded that there was no evidence supporting one kind of mentoring over another. For example, researchers did not support classroom-based mentoring over full-time mentoring positions or vice versa. Figure 4.2 compares the two types of mentors/coaches.

*The research that supports coaching as successful professional development for novices and struggling teachers is based on peer coaching (Joyce & Showers, 1983). These researchers and many others are clear that the best help comes from people who see themselves as equals. It can be difficult (although not impossible) for full-time mentors or coaches to maintain peer relationships with novices and struggling teachers. It can be especially difficult if full-time mentors or coaches seem to have more power and authority than the teachers they help. It can also be difficult for novices or struggling teachers to see a person who has exceptional experience, skills, and knowledge (e.g., a master teacher) as their equal. Even if the exceptional person is respectful and acknowledges the equality of the person being helped, both people in the relationship may grant the helper more power and authority, especially if that person also has a role that takes him or her out of the classroom. Identification as a "classroom" teacher can be a great equalizer, and designation as a full-time mentor or coach with an office can affect that equality.

Mentors Were Classroom-Based, But Other Helpers Were Not

As a struggling school, Lincoln was allotted many layers of specialist helpers; however, mentors were classroom-based except for two of my participants who, as you may recall, were both mentors and coaches. They had offices and could schedule their own time. Other specialists from the district office who were concerned with testing achievement often visited the teachers and collegial partners at Lincoln to check up on them. The school had other helpers as well, including curriculum (not content) coaches, assistant principals in charge of instruction (APIs), and department chairs.

Figure 4.2 Full-Time Mentors or Coaches vs. Classroom-Based Mentors or Coaches

Full-Time Mentors or Coaches	Classroom-Based Mentors or Coaches
Have more control of their time to research and learn useful skills and are not constrained by limited planning time	Available time aligns with other classroom teachers who are constrained by classroom responsibilities and have limited planning time
Have an office in which to meet privately with novices or struggling teachers	Have the same spaces as their colleagues
Are a less expensive way to provide in-school professional development (e.g., full-time mentors or coaches can learn new skills and content and bring ideas back to the school vs. hiring expensive outside trainers)	Are less expensive if mentors or coaches receive only a small stipend or no extra money
A way to acknowledge quality teachers by giving them a special role	A way to keep quality teachers in the classroom
*Have more difficulty maintaining equal status with classroom teachers	Are more likely to have an equal status with classroom teachers
Have more access to school leaders and align with them in terms of control of their time and space	Have more access to the status of the teaching professionals at the school

All but the department chairs had their own offices and control of their time. Department chairs did have an extra planning period.

One mentor/coach, Mrs. Herman, seemed to be able to maintain her "peer" status; other coaches were not as successful. Unfortunately, administrators and district leaders required Mrs. Herman to join with a specialist coach from the district when she came to visit. On one occasion, according to Mrs. Herman, this district coach's evaluative stance greatly upset Mrs. Herman's mentee, Mrs. Stewart, who had a "melt-down" and called in sick the next day. Mrs. Herman had a hard time trying to convince Mrs. Stewart that the critique of her work offered by the district coach was just a suggestion and did not represent a negative evaluation.

Tip #2: School leaders may consider the benefits of classroom-based mentors or coaches versus full-time practitioners at their school. If districts require schools to receive help from specialists, they can help administrators and teachers understand that districts design these positions to help them rather than evaluate them. If collegial partners are full-time specialists rather than classroom teachers, they should make special efforts to convey a sense of equality by sharing responsibilities with the teachers they help. When I was an academic facilitator and a literacy coach, I was committed to connecting myself as closely as possible to the same responsibilities and within the same constraints that the classroom teachers had. In order to do this, I co-planned lessons with individuals and teams, team-taught or observed as many teachers as I could every day, occasionally provided direct services for students that teams asked me to assist in to help both the students and the teachers, and took on a variety of teaching duties before, during, and after school. I experienced a level of commitment and responsibility that was somewhere between that of a classroom teacher and an administrator. Because I was in and out of lots of classrooms and heard the concerns of administrative teams as they did their best to respond to district pressure, I was able to see the global issues with which administrative teams dealt. On the other hand, I was also able to understand the concerns of classroom teachers, and I empathized with the pressures they experienced as well. Full-time partners who wish to convey a sense of equality could do some of the things I did, but the most important thing is to encourage those they help to approach them with any concerns about how they work together. This "open door" approach may only work through word of mouth so that if some teachers do come to partners with concerns, and they like the way they handle them, then their open door gains credibility. However, if partners say the door is open but teachers find that those are only words and not a reality, then few, if any, will walk through that door.

Contrasting Helping Relationships

In an effort to improve schools and, in some cases, to retain teachers, decision makers have looked to formally assigned mentors and coaches for help. Novice and struggling teachers can find help when they join a team of teachers, when they coach a sport or oversee an activity, or when other professional teachers make a point of reaching out in friendship to welcome them into the profession. Some teachers even receive help from family members who are or have been in the profession. Administrators and district specialists also have the goal of helping new and struggling teachers. With all of these helpers it is sometimes difficult to distinguish mentoring or coaching from other forms of help. It could be useful to distinguish these roles from other helping roles in order to possibly (but not always) avert misunderstandings that could have a negative impact on collegial partnerships. If these roles and responsibilities are not clear, the relationship could have an "identity crisis."

Mentors Had an Identity at Lincoln High School

When I determined the eight dominant descriptors for mentors at Lincoln, I made a table to differentiate mentors from other helpers. (See Figure 4.3, page 82.) By doing this, I also was able to better identify the roles of those helping relationships with which I contrasted mentoring.

This table provided further information that mentors at Lincoln had a distinct relationship with their mentees. It is interesting that Mrs. Herman, who was both a mentor and a coach qualified as a mentor; however, Mrs. Stanley, who was also a coach and a mentor, did not. One major reason she did not qualify is that she was in the building only two days a week, so she did not have the daily contact with mentees that the other mentors did. Additionally, her alignment with Mrs. Lawson, her mentee, was questionable, especially during the first year of their relationship.

Tip #3: School leaders and teachers need to understand that in a culture of helping, everyone helps each other; however, each helping relationship has its own identity. For example, the concepts of mentoring and coaching fit into a category that linguists refer to as "floating signifiers" (Cary, 2004). The term *floating signifier* refers to those terms that seem to have clear definitions, but that, on closer examination, include many views of the concept. School leaders who realize the terms *mentoring* and *coaching* could mean different things to different people will make a point of having conversations with their stakeholders that attempt to reach consensus about how those implementing the concepts work together.

They might also recognize that each type of helping relationship is important, and that mentoring and coaching help differs from the help offered by a friend or a family member. One of the ways stakeholders might learn to differentiate mentors from coaches and other kinds of helpers is to ask the teachers and those in helping roles these two questions:

- ♦ What distinguishes mentoring from coaching from each other at this school?
- ♦ How are these two more formal modes of helping different from the informal help of professional friends and family?

Figure 4.3 Descriptors Differentiating Helpers in the Novice's Network of Support

Descriptors	M–N	C–N	F–N	Fa–N	A–N	Cn–N	P–N	O–N
Superior knowledge of the school culture	X	X			X	X	X	
Superior experience teaching challenging students	X	X					X	
Respected, empowered, and trusted by school leadership but aligned with novice	X	X			X		X	X
Admired each other's practices	X		X					
A one-on-one commitment	X							
Daily contact	X		X					
Collaborated and shared ideas and materials	X		X				X	X
Could not stop administrators from dismissing novices	X	X	X	X		X	X	X

Source: Reproduced from Waterman (2012, p. 106).

Note: Mentor–Novice (M–N); Coach–Novice (C–N); Professional friends–Novice (F–N); Family who were educators–Novice (Fa–N); Administrator–Novice (A–N); Counselor–Novice (Cn–N); Professional Learning Community–Novice (P–N); Other designated helping professionals such as district coaches (O–N)

No two schools are alike, and schools can have different ideas about how to distinguish one role from the other. From my perspective, mentors can provide coaching and coaches can provide mentoring, but these processes are different from each other and stakeholders may want to make sure novices and struggling teachers get some of both. Stakeholders may consider having at least one meeting to help their school community determine exactly how mentoring, coaching, and other kinds of helping work at their school. Leaders might cite some of the literature about these processes and use one of the concept development frameworks (e.g., Hilda Taba's "Concept Development") I describe in the Activities section of this chapter.

Saving Time and Money

Decision makers and school leaders concerned with saving time and money may consider the idea of mentoring and coaching "from the classroom." In the current education climate, decision makers seem to believe that paying for outside consultants is the way to improve schools. Findings from my study and others challenge this belief. Special consultants and professional developers can be expensive, and it is difficult for those who are "special" to function as peers with those they intend to help; therefore, money can be wasted on people who may have no effect on school improvement.

Mentoring and coaching from the classroom can be a good way to provide professional development for all teachers. When a school employs several special consultants to conduct professional development, they tend to take teachers' time and to be less relevant to their needs. The need for additional training meetings can be difficult for some teachers who resent having to constantly take time for professional training sessions. Coaches and mentors may better understand and accommodate their teachers' training needs and scheduling issues.

Activities

All of these activities might be useful for two people to do together or for groups of people to do in pairs and then share with the larger group, such as a faculty meeting.

Identity Circles

This activity, adapted from Bonner Curriculum (n.d.), is intended to help mentors/coaches and teachers explore in some depth who they are (i.e., their identities). Participants will need a pen or pencil, blank note cards, and a sheet of blank paper or an already drawn "Identity Circle" handout (page 86).

Step 1: Due to the potentially sensitive nature of this kind of work, it is a good idea to bring participants gradually into the idea of sharing personal information. One way to start people talking about who they are is to have them discuss the origins of their names with their partners. Participants might talk about their full names or parts of them. They might explain the origins and their significance. If you are leading this activity in a faculty meeting or another kind of group, you may model the kind of sharing you would like for participants to emulate. For example, I might share with the group that my name is Sheryn. My mother, who was from South Carolina, did not like the way southerners pronounced Sharon with a long ***a,*** so she changed the spelling to solve that problem. Unfortunately, her idea created problems for me, because ***no one*** else spells the name that way. As I have grown older, I have come to appreciate that my mother, who is now deceased, wanted to be creative and wanted her daughter to have a special name. Now instead of feeling irritated by her decision, I have learned to value my name's unique spelling.

Step 2: Introduce the basic ideas of the sharing process, which should include the following:

- Participation is voluntary.
- All participants agree to do whatever it takes to make the space for sharing a safe place.
- All participants are committed to speaking honestly about themselves.
- The structure of the activity will be maintained through collaboration.

Step 3: Participants either draw their own or get a copy of the "Identity Circle" handout.

Step 4: Participants write their name in the circle in the middle of the "Identity Circle," and then they should take about five minutes to write words that describe their identity in each of eight spokes that surround the circle. Facilitators should model this process. For example, I would explain that I would write *Sheryn* in the middle. Some of my one-word descriptors are "mother," "wife," "consultant," and "author," and my phrases are "I have a Ph.D." and "I am a Licensed Professional Counselor."

Step 5: When participants have completed all eight spokes surrounding their name, they should take turns sharing for three to five minutes about what they wrote. Facilitators may ask participants to organize their sharing by asking them to talk about specific categories such as:

- I am most proud of …
- I am most happy about …
- I am presently struggling with …
- I was surprised by … .
- I want the group to know this about me …

It is extremely important that participants share without being interrupted. Their partners or other participants should not ask questions or say anything, even if it is encouraging.

Step 6: After everyone has shared, partners or group members should have a conversation that addresses these kinds of questions:

- How did you feel about participating in this process?
- Were you surprised by anything we have talked about today?
- How might this process help mentors/coaches and teachers work together?
- How might this process help larger groups, such as our team or our entire school?

Step 7: Get a blank card and write on one side the answer to this question: What did you learn from this activity? On the other side write the answer to this question: How might this activity affect your future actions? *Do not identify yourself on the card.* Give your card to facilitators or share your card with your partner if you are doing this in pairs.

Identity Circles Handout

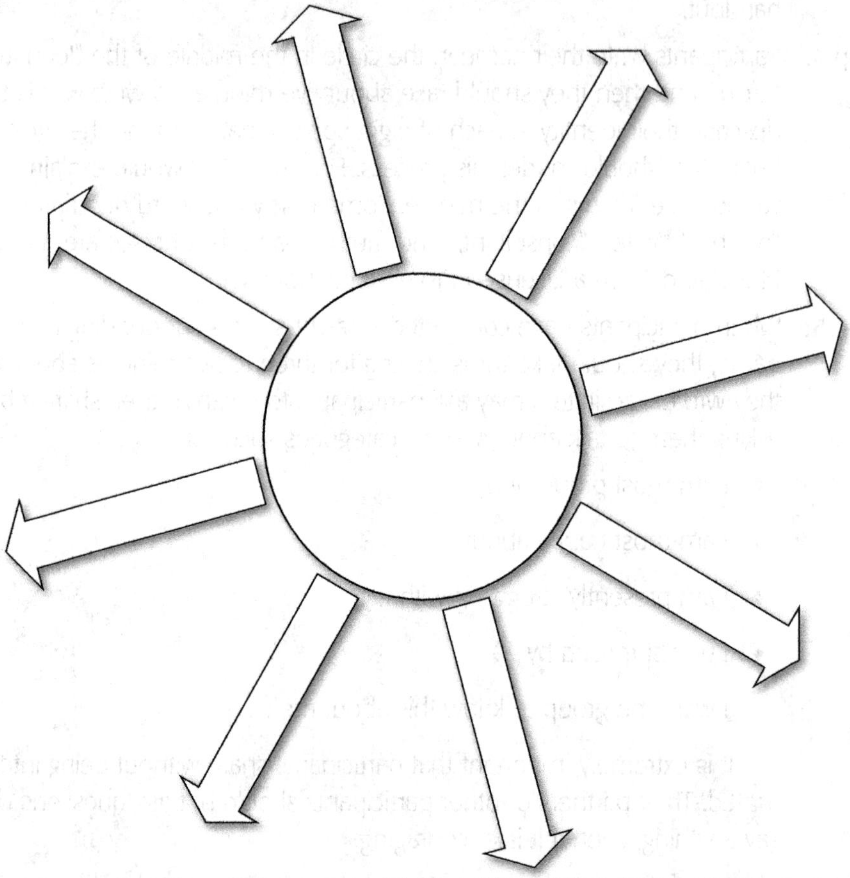

Source: Adapted from Bonner Curriculum (n.d.).

StarPower

A game called "StarPower" demonstrates how unbalanced power can affect those who have it and those who do not (Simulation Training Systems, 2011). In this game, power is divided into three levels: highest, middle, and lowest. Those who play the game usually learn experientially that those with the most power control the game and are unwilling to share their power with those who do not have it. Those who are in the middle are constantly trying to become members of the power group, but that group looks down on them and on those with the least power. Those with the least power become apathetic unless they are energized by thinking of ways to cheat or rebel against those in power (Meadows, n.d.).

Some schools may reflect this kind of unbalanced power. For example, a school may convey the highest power to principals and superintendents, middle-level power to administrative team members and mentor/coach specialists, and the least power to classroom teachers. In this kind of school, teachers' classrooms might also reflect this structure in which the teacher, who has the least power in the school, exerts the most power in the classroom. Successful students gain middle-level power, and struggling students have the least power. One can see why the teachers in schools with unbalanced power might feel apathetic or rebellious, and how struggling students might also feel apathetic and rebellious in their classrooms.

Schools might experience the benefits of sharing power so that everyone feels welcome to contribute as best they can to the process of learning. Sharing power does not mean that everyone has the same role; it just means that everyone is responsible for making the school work for them and for the school community. A school community where everyone is valued and empowered is a place of energy and achievement rather than apathy and rebellion.

What Is Your Brand?

Branding has become an important aspect of describing the identity of an organization for marketing purposes. It can be fun and informative to create a brand that describes the identities of mentors/coaches and teachers and/or for departments and teams. One idea is to develop what is called a "brand essence," which appeals to the heart and to the mind and is a timeless expression of identity. Brand essence is expressed by using the following formula: adjective, adjective, noun. For example: "Starbucks's brand essence: Rewarding everyday moments." (Daye, n.d., p. 1). Note that this idea is an update on the idea of creating "slogans." Participants will need markers and poster board, card stock, or a large line-free note card.

Step 1: Talk about the concept of branding. Tell participants that they will be thinking of a brand for themselves (or their teams) that captures their identity and that might appeal to others.

Step 2: Ask participants to think of an adjective, adjective, noun phrase that describes them (or their team).

Step 3: Use that phrase to design a graphic that includes or describes those words and draw it on the paper provided. (See example below.)

My Brand

Flexible, expressive writer

Step 4: Share brands with each other or with teams and provide an opportunity for participants to talk about what they learned from the experience and how they might use it in the future.

Identity Story

Creating an identity story can be an interesting way to learn about one's positive traits and to share oneself with others (Denning, 2004). An identity story, which can be rather short, is not the same as an autobiography. The identity story has the elements of a good story: a basic situation that includes a setting, characters, and what's going on; rising action that includes a major conflict; a climax that occurs when the conflict is solved; and falling action or resolution that shows the effects of solving the conflict on the rest of the story. The storyteller is the hero or heroine of the identity story. Participants create their stories using the following steps:

Step 1: Crafting a Basic Situation. Participants place themselves in their school and describe events on a typical school day. For example, I might begin an identity story this way: *Mrs. Waterman walked into Lincoln High School one Monday morning after school had been in session for about one quarter. She greeted her fellow teachers and said "hello" to a stylishly dressed group of diverse students who were socializing before the bell rang. Mrs. Waterman's school was in the heart of the city and the students who attended spoke about thirty languages. She had been teaching at Lincoln for twelve years, was respected by administrators and colleagues, and consequently, administrators had asked her to mentor a young teacher, Ms. Smith.*

In this example, I included the following:

- ♦ Characters: Myself as the main character (twelve-year veteran), Ms. Smith (novice) as another major character, and several minor characters including colleagues and students, whom I described as diverse.
- ♦ Setting (Place and Time): Lincoln High School, which I described as being "downtown." The time was at the end of the first quarter of the school year.
- ♦ Basic Situation: We were nearing the end of first quarter and as a well-respected member of the faculty, I was mentoring a first-year teacher, Ms. Smith.

Step 2: Determining the Conflict. Participants think of a conflict that grows as the story progresses (rising action), which they can solve in the climax. For example: *When Mrs. Waterman got to her classroom, she saw Ms. Smith standing at her door. She appeared to be waiting for her, and she looked as if she had been crying. Mrs. Waterman walked up to her and asked her what was wrong. Ms. Smith told her that she had received an email from administration telling her that if she did not get her required paperwork in by this afternoon, she would be in trouble. Ms. Smith said, "I am so far behind, I am thinking of quitting."*

In this example I presented the **conflict,** which was that Ms. Smith had gotten behind in her paperwork and was thinking of resigning.

Step 3: **Describing the Rising Action.** Participants use their explanation of how they solved the conflict in order to show who they are, where they came from, and where they are headed. In other words, they reveal their identities by the way they solve problems. For example: *Mrs. Waterman put her arm around Ms. Smith and said, "Can we talk during planning? I have to set up my lesson, but I promise you that we can work this out. Just take a deep breath and get through first period." Ms. Smith agreed to hold on for their planning period. During first period, Mrs. Waterman thought about how she was going to help Ms. Smith. She recalled how she had struggled as a first-year teacher and how her own mentor had let her down. She was determined not to let Ms. Smith down, because she knew how hard the first year could be, and she was the kind of person who tried her best to be accepting and caring rather than judgmental and critical.*

When Mrs. Waterman and Ms. Smith got together, Mrs. Waterman took time to listen and clearly understand Ms. Smith's problem. She discovered that Ms. Smith had not kept good records of students' work, which had created a paperwork emergency as they approached the end of the quarter. Instead of offering to do the work for Ms. Smith, which Mrs. Waterman believed would not be helpful to her growth as a professional, she showed Ms. Smith her own record-keeping methods and encouraged her to find a better way to keep her own records. Beyond offering a concrete solution to the paperwork problem, Mrs. Waterman told Ms. Smith about her own struggles as a first-year teacher and explained that all teachers run into problems. Mrs. Waterman found specific reasons to compliment Ms. Smith and encouraged her not to give up.

In this example, I presented the **rising action,** which helped to convey the positive aspects of my identity. It showed that I was compassionate, empathetic, accepting, skilled, and appreciative.

Step 4: **Reaching a Climax.** At this point, the story should show how the conflict is resolved. For example: *Ms. Smith seemed to brighten and to find the energy to correct the paperwork problem. Best of all, she decided not to resign.*

In this example, I showed that the way in which I had approached Ms. Smith helped her change her attitude so that she could solve her own problem and stay in the profession.

Step 5: **Resolution.** In the resolution, participants describe what happens after the problem is solved. This part of the story shows the part of my identity that looks to the future and shows a direction in which I am headed. For example: *One day toward the end of the year, Mrs. Waterman walked toward her classroom and again saw Ms. Smith standing by her door.*

This time, although Ms. Smith looked like she wanted to talk to Mrs. Waterman, she had a smile on her face. "What's up, Ms. Smith?" Mrs. Waterman asked. Ms. Smith had found out that one of her struggling students had done exceptionally well on his end-of-year exams. Mrs. Waterman congratulated her and said. "It's a good thing you were here to make a difference!" Mrs. Waterman believed that it was important that as a veteran she should help to bring new teachers into the profession and that keeping good teachers meant helping students achieve.

In this example, my **resolution** showed that both Ms. Smith and I had grown in our commitment to the future of the teaching profession and to student achievement.

Step 6: **Sharing Stories.** Participants may share the parts of their stories along the process or wait until the end to share them. This should be a powerful experience. Participants might talk about what they learned from creating their stories and if they had any surprises. They might also talk about what they learned from hearing others' stories.

Concept Development Ideas

Mentoring and coaching are specific concepts that partners or groups might explore using a variety of concept/vocabulary development ideas. For example, teachers might use the following:

- Frayer Model of Vocabulary Development. For graphic organizer and directions, see http://worksheetworks.com/miscellanea/graphic-organizers/frayer.html.
- Hilda Taba's Model of Concept Formation. For directions, see http://edutechwiki.unige.ch/en/Taba_teaching_strategy_model.
- Jerome Brunner's Model of Concept Development. For explanations, see http://edutechwiki.unige.ch/en/Concept_learning.
- Concept Mapping. For directions, see http://graphic.org/concept.html.

Using any of these methods can help mentors/coaches and teachers better understand the unique identity of these various roles in their schools. It is important that decision makers who hire them and teachers who use their services understand that those roles are unique for every setting in which they are employed. There is no one right way to do mentoring and coaching, and no one way that these roles are implemented in schools. Using a process like the ones mentioned here will help clarify relationships and responsibilities.

CHAPTER 5

Five Tips About Being Adaptable and Flexible

Collegial partnerships adjust and are flexible in order to be able to handle a wide variety of school conflicts.

Instability—Adjusting and Adapting

Even though mentor and coach roles have specific identities due to closed boundaries, their energy is unstable so that they are constantly moving and adjusting to their surroundings. According to Davis and Sumara (2006), complex systems are "unstable" and "exist far from equilibrium," which means they do not "operate in balance," and they are in constant motion or they will die (p. 6). For example, in a human system, if the heart stops pumping blood through the body, the person dies; in a social system, if the system stops responding to its environment, it can cease to exist or become a different kind of system. Just as being closed creates identity, being open and in motion also creates it. For example, if couples stop dancing, they no longer exist as dancing couples; they become something else—two separate people who may be standing together but functioning separately. Figure 5.1 (page 92) shows how collegial partners seem to *adapt* to each other, to organizational changes, and to student behaviors. Interestingly, being able to adapt is one of the most important processes that facilitates the capacity of partnerships to survive, grow, and learn.

Figure 5.1 Adapting

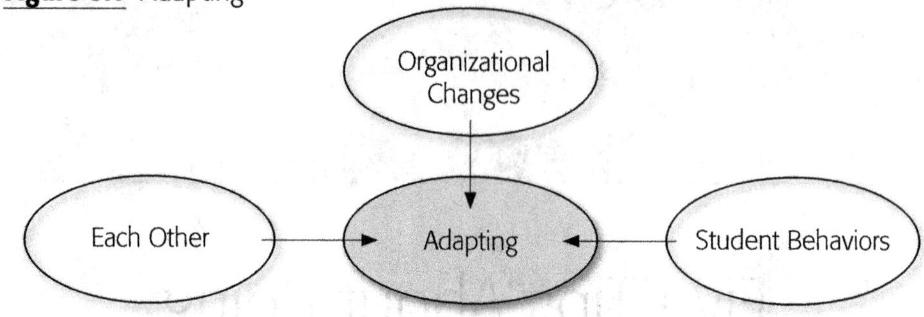

Adapting to Each Other

One of the tasks of developing any kind of human relationship is that those in the relationship need to be able to adapt to each other. If that does not happen, the relationship will most likely end. Because the kinds of adjustments one might make with a work-related relationship differ from adjustments involved in the development of a personal relationship, novice teachers or struggling teachers may feel somewhat constrained in their ability to honestly express themselves so that trust is affected. The ability to trust each other influences how adjustments proceed and the types of adjustments that might lead to deepening the relationship. Some of the ways collegial partners adapt to one another include acceptance of communication styles, demeanor, behaviors under stress, trustworthiness, relationship skills, maturity, skill and knowledge levels, and level of flexibility. The kinds of roles accepted by partners also have an impact on how they are able to adapt to each other.

Trust Closes the Gap

At Lincoln, collegial partners seemed mostly well-adjusted to each other. When I interviewed mentors and novices together I felt clearly that strong relationships had developed over the short time they had been together. In most cases they had differences in communication styles, maturity levels, skill and knowledge levels, and relationship skills, but they seemed to trust each other, which closed many of the gaps between them. One of the most successful relationships was between Mr. Hansen (novice) and Mrs. Truitt (mentor), who had fundamentally different personalities. For example, she saw herself as outspoken and aggressive, and he seemed soft-spoken and laid-back. Despite these differences, the challenges they had faced together since they met on the school bus trip seemed to have deepened their relationship.

Tip #1: Collegial partners will need to make many adjustments in order to get along. However, if they can trust each other, they will be able to adapt in order to develop a strong relationship. They can use some trust-building activities from Chapter 2, such as "Whom Do You Trust?" in the Activities section of the chapter. School leaders and partnerships who understand the importance of trust will model trustworthiness themselves. For example, they will personally avoid criticizing one teacher to another, gossiping about teachers to other teachers and administrators, soliciting gossip from others, and listening to others gossip or criticize. School leaders can send a strong message that a teacher's reputations at their school will not be at the mercy of the rumor mill. At the beginning of the school year and periodically though the year, school leaders might say, "At this school, we do not talk behind the backs of those with whom we may have a problem. We talk to their faces, with respect."

Organizational Changes

Collegial partnerships work in educational environments that are complex and therefore unstable. Two areas that seemed to be the most difficult for partnerships in terms of adapting are accountability and paperwork. In the current educational climate, educators from all levels are accountable for student achievement. Policy makers, district leaders, and school leaders constantly look for ways to improve schools; therefore, they frequently make changes in programs and policies they hope will make a difference, especially in struggling schools. These changes, which can come at any time during the school year, can be difficult for new and struggling teachers who are sometimes doing all they can to learn how to adjust to their school. Frequent organizational changes can make mentoring/coaching more challenging. Paperwork, which is often generated based on organizational changes, can seem excessive from the perspective of novices and struggling teachers. It can be challenging for mentors and coaches to help them add paperwork to the many other tasks with which they are dealing.

Going to Bat for Teachers

The mentors and coaches at Lincoln often found themselves defending novices around accountability and paperwork issues. At Lincoln, if teachers' students did not score well on end-of-grade tests, district policy required those teachers to go into a special designation in which other educators closely observed and monitored their work. For instance, the district required them to turn in detailed lesson plans on a regular basis, which was more than other teachers were required to do. These teachers also had to complete paperwork that documented their teaching strategies and the efforts they made to help students achieve. Although these requirements may have been necessary to protect students' opportunities to learn, in some cases novices seemed overwhelmed with paperwork and it was difficult for their collegial partners to help them.

> **Tip #2:** School leaders and decision makers should assess the effects of organizational changes on their novices and struggling teachers. If they find that the school improvement initiatives have created additional paperwork that is time consuming and/or difficult, they might give novices and struggling teachers extra time or extra help to complete the work. For example, teams of teachers might get together to handle paperwork in an atmosphere of camaraderie. If they discover that they have a large amount of paperwork to complete, such as sections of standardized tests, "Personalized Instructional Plans," or parent contact logs, they could plan a "Documentation Day" during which they bring snacks and work together in a social atmosphere. Those who are struggling with the paperwork can feel the support of their fellow teachers and mentors/coaches.

Student Behaviors

Students' behaviors can be challenging, and collegial partners may need to help mentees or struggling teachers adapt. Students (and sometimes their parents) can exhibit behaviors that take time and experience to learn and some novices and struggling teachers may have significant difficulties adapting to those behaviors. Collegial partners, if they are to be helpful regarding these challenges, not only need to have their own excellent skills in adapting to student challenges but also need to understand the problems that novices/struggling teachers are having with their students. If partners do not understand how student behaviors require novices and struggling teachers to adapt, they probably cannot help them very much. Another area in which novices and struggling teachers may need to adapt to student behaviors is when the system requires them to teach a specific curriculum. Sometimes that curriculum does not closely match the needs of certain students, and it can take considerable experience to be able to adapt the curriculum to their needs. In addition to helping novices and struggling teachers adapt to challenging student behaviors, partners may also need to help mentors or struggling teachers learn to adapt curricula to students' needs.

Challenging Student Behaviors at Lincoln

All of the novice teachers who participated in my study taught students who exhibited challenging behaviors. Fortunately, all of their collegial partners had experience adapting to these challenging behaviors, and in several cases, they were able to help novices adapt to them as well. It was difficult for Mrs. Stewart, a novice who taught a specific curriculum, to adapt that curriculum to the needs of her special students. These students had difficulty adapting to some of the curriculum requirements, and Mrs. Stewart did not always have enough experience to be able to adapt these requirements to meet her students' needs. Fortunately, her mentor/coach, Mrs. Herman, and another more experienced colleague, Mrs. Anderson, were able to help Mrs. Stewart better adapt her curriculum to the needs of her students. Mrs. Anderson also helped Mrs. Stewart understand that it was all right and even preferable that she use teaching materials that she enjoyed. Mrs. Stewart realized that because her students could tell that she was bored by textbook materials, they also responded negatively to those materials. Using more engaging materials improved teacher-student relationships and Mrs. Herman remarked in one of the interviews that Mrs. Stewart was no longer getting push back from the students and for some of them, she was their favorite teacher.

> **Tip #3:** Collegial partners and school leaders may consider prioritizing strategies for addressing the needs of challenging students. They can collaborate with novices or struggling teachers to explore skills that help these teachers adjust to these students who need their understanding. Even if the school has scripted or structured teaching programs, partnerships should consider evaluating the effectiveness of standardized programs and possibly adapting them to meet local needs. School leaders and partnerships might become familiar with many of the resources for differentiating instruction and assessment. I have written several (e.g., Northey, 2005; Waterman, 2007; Waterman, 2009a; Waterman, 2009b; Waterman 2010a; Waterman, 2010b). Partnerships might also refer to the "Pyramid of Interventions" (Cincinnati Pubic Schools, 2006) or other models for addressing the needs of all students. Novices or struggling teachers from a variety of pre-service experiences may or may not have had access to a wide variety of strategies for dealing with challenging students. Partners who have had success with these students could provide important perspectives about what worked best for them.

Being Flexible

Not only are collegial partnerships unstable, but they are also ambiguously bounded, which means that they are *flexible* in order to be open to influences or disturbances from forces outside or within the relationship. Disturbances from within the relationship often come from differences between people or role confusion. Outside disturbances usually come from other teachers, students, family members, administrators, and district staff. Some outside and inside disturbances are welcome and some are unwelcome. These welcome and unwelcome disturbances are also known as *triggers*, and these can *trigger* emergent responses from complex systems, such as partnerships. For example, a problem with a student could trigger a negative response from a novice or struggling teacher, which could make it necessary for a partner to help with that response. Being ambiguously bounded allows for flexibility, which makes it more likely that mentors or coaches and novices or struggling teachers can respond effectively to each other. (See Figure 5.2.)

Figure 5.2 Flexible

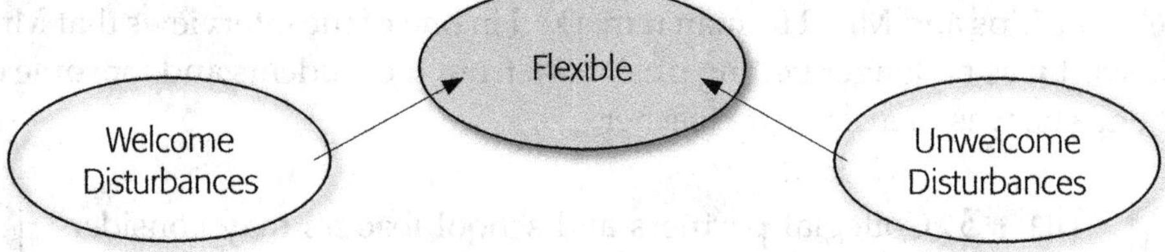

Welcome Disturbances

Teachers are notorious for "borrowing" or "stealing" ideas from each other. Many of them welcome new ideas about how to teach a topic. They may also welcome constructive feedback from collegial partners regarding their teaching practices. Novices or struggling teachers who are open to disturbing the status quo of their practices have a better chance to grow and improve. Ideas can come from a wide variety of sources—not only from mentors and coaches but also from knowledgeable family members and professional friends. These ideas can greatly enrich the practices of new and struggling teachers.

Don't Leave Anything Lying Around

Most of the novices and struggling teachers I interviewed welcomed teaching ideas from a variety of sources. For example, several of my participants often consulted family members who were educators. All of my research participants were open to ideas from professional friends, administrators, district personnel, teachers in other departments, and teammates; however, they seemed most likely to welcome new ideas if they asked for them or if someone offered them as choices rather than mandates. The novices at Lincoln also liked to believe that they had ideas to offer the veteran teachers. For example, one novice, Mrs. Lawson, found it especially rewarding to share ideas with fellow members of her professional learning community, and she felt upset when a veteran said she was not interested in some of the materials the novice offered her. The best example of openness to gathering new ideas from others came from Mrs. Herman, who said that teachers had better not leave anything in the work room or she was liable to steal it!

> **Tip #4:** Mentors and coaches should understand that novices and struggling teachers welcome interesting new teaching ideas if they ask for them or if someone offers them as choices rather than mandates. Novices and struggling teachers may also be more interested in implementing ideas from mentors and coaches if they are willing to try new ideas that novices or struggling teachers bring to the relationship. In other words, ideas can come from both sides of the relationship rather than one-way from mentors and coaches to novices and struggling teachers.

Unwelcome Disturbances

Flexibility is the key to functioning within a complex social system like a school, and most teachers understand that they need to be able to accept unwelcome disturbances if they want to be successful. Unwelcome disturbances can come from students who have challenging needs, new initiatives to understand and implement, and additional responsibilities to fit into the schedule. Even though these kinds of disturbances can be unwelcome, they are not necessarily negative. However, the fact that teachers did not choose these disturbances makes them more difficult to accept and to incorporate into practice.

Flexibility Is the Key to Survival

Mrs. Herman told me the first time I met her that the way to make it at Lincoln was to be flexible. She knew what she was talking about because she had been a teacher for more than thirty years, and she had been at Lincoln longer than any of the principals with whom she had worked. Mrs. Herman understood, and she helped her mentees/struggling teachers understand, that the students at Lincoln *needed* their teachers to be flexible to adjust to them, that every teacher *needed* to learn to implement new initiatives, and that the school *needed* them to accept additional responsibilities into their schedules. Willingness to meet these needs made the difference between those who made it and those who did not.

> **Tip #5:** School decision makers and collegial partnerships might use activities such as "Who Moved My Cheese?" to explore how flexible they are responding to the inevitable disturbances inherent in all schools. They might also use "Welcome and Unwelcome Experiences" to talk about how school changes affect them.

Activities

Whom Do You Trust?

This activity is useful in small groups or with partners, and it could help those who participate talk about what trust means to them. Participants need a pencil and the "Whom Do You Trust?" handout. (See completed example.)

Step 1: Tell participants that they will be thinking about whom they trust and exploring some reasons why. They might share their findings with a partner or in a small group.

Step 2: Ask participants to complete #1 of the handout.

Step 3: For #2 on the handout, participants might work on their own or with a partner to create ten sentences or phrases that describe the traits that make these people trustworthy.

Step 3: Rank order the list by transferring the sentences into the table on the handout.

Step 4: Make sure participants understand the rating process as described on the handout and encourage them to first rate themselves.

Step 5: Encourage participants to share whatever they are comfortable sharing with each other. Ask them to talk about new learning, especially surprises.

Example: Whom Do You Trust?

1. Make a list of some (or all) of the people you trust.
   David, Sarah, Rick, Joy, Brenda, Madeleine, Nancy, Amy, Jeff, Jeanne, Billy, Gene, Anne, Kathy, Betsy
2. Create at least ten sentences or phrases that explain why you trust these people.
   1. I can say how I feel about most things
   2. They would not knowingly try to hurt me.
   3. They care about my well-being.
   4. They do not judge me or criticize me.
   5. I can be myself with them.
   6. They respect me.
   7. When I am with them I can relax.
   8. I know they enjoy my company and like to be with me.
   9. We can talk about all kinds of topics.
   10. I know they won't gossip about me.
3. Rank the sentences as you transfer them into the table below (10=highest; 1=lowest). Make sure to order them with 10 being the highest.

#	Traits	Self	P1	P2
10	With this person I can say how I feel about most things.	10	10	
9	I know this person won't gossip about me.	9	9	9
8	This person cares about my well-being.	8	8	8
7	This person respects me.		7	
6	I can be myself with this person.	6	6	
5	When I am with this person I can relax.		5	
4	This person would not knowingly hurt me.			
3	This person does not judge me or criticize me.			
2	I know this person enjoys my company and likes to be with me.	2		
1	This person and I can talk about all kinds of topics.	1	1	1
Totals		36	46	18

4. Using the table, first rate yourself and then rate at least two other people with whom you are in a helping relationship. The rating process goes as follows: (1) If the trait is true of the person you are rating, write down the number in the left column. If the trait is not true of the person, leave the cell blank. (2) Add up the numbers in each of the columns to get a score. The higher the score, the more you trust the person.
5. Share whatever you are comfortable sharing with a partner or with the group.

Adapting to Change: Who Moved My Cheese?

This activity is based on Spencer Johnson's bestselling book, *Who Moved My Cheese?* Applying his premise about change and the various types of reactions we have to it, use the following template to explore the effect of a welcome or unwelcome change in someone's life, a school, a district, or the national culture of education reform. See the completed example below.

Step 1: Think of a change that could be a metaphor for the "cheese" that someone might move or plan to move that has an impact on you. This change could be one that affects you, your school, your district, or the national culture of education with which you are dealing or plan to deal.

Step 2: Insert on the line provided a word or phrase that describes that change.

Step 3: After you have filled in the blanks, first reflect by yourself, and then, if possible, share your ideas with another person or a small group.

Step 4: After you have reflected and/or talked about the effects of this change, rate yourself according to which of the characters in Part II of *Who Moved My Cheese?* best describes how you are dealing with or plan to deal with that change.

Step 5: Share your answers with a partner or in a small group and talk about what you learned about yourself and your colleagues by participating in this activity.

***Example:* Who Moved My ________________ (Cheese)?**
I. The Cheese ____________________ (describe what is changing)
1. "Change happens. They keep moving the professional development process." (the cheese)
2. "Anticipate change. Get ready for the professional development process (cheese) to move."
3. "Monitor change. Smell the professional development process (cheese) often so you know when it is getting old."
4. "Adapt to change quickly. The more quickly you let go of the old professional development process (describe the way it used to be), the sooner you can enjoy the new professional development process (cheese)."
5. "Change. Move with the new professional development process (cheese)."
6. "Enjoy change. Savor the adventure and the taste of the new professional development process (cheese)."
7. "Be ready to quickly change again and again. They keep moving the professional development process (describe new possible changes)."

(continued)

II. Parts of Myself

Put a check by the mouse name or names (i.e., part of yourself) that best describe how you are dealing with this professional development process (cheese).

√ Sniff—I am finding out as much as I can about this change and how I, my team, my school, etc. will react or is reacting.

√ Scurry—I am planning to or have moved quickly into action around this change.

__ Hem—I am denying and resisting this change because it is uncomfortable for me and I am afraid it will lead to something even worse if we have to implement it as it is now.

__ Haw—I am learning to adapt to this change because I can see how it will lead to better outcomes.

What part of me (e.g., Sniff, Scurry, Hem, and/ or Haw) is reacting to the new professional development process (cheese)? Why? I am dealing with the new professional development process like Sniff and Scurry because I am curious about it and because I may have to help novices and struggling teachers learn to participate in it.

Source: Adapted from Johnson (1998, p. 12, 74)

Welcome and Unwelcome Experiences

Step 1: Take a few minutes to reflect on some key experiences you have had since the beginning of the school year.

Step 2: Categorize them as "welcome" or "unwelcome" and briefly explain what happened. Next put how you felt about each experience.

Step 3: Reflect on your categorization and feelings and/or share with a partner or a small group.

Step 4: Reflect on the basis for those feelings.

Step 5: Talk about your responses to these experiences and if you are satisfied with them or if you are interested in changing them.

It could be useful to talk about both kinds of experiences on a regular basis and to determine how your responses have changed or not and why. This exercise can help mentors/coaches and novices/struggling teachers take a look at novice/ struggling teachers' experiences and their feelings about them. They might have complex conversations about how to deal with unwelcome experiences so that they determine helpful strategies.

Example: Welcome and Unwelcome Disturbances

Welcome	Unwelcome
1. **Small-group orientation for my team**—Helped me learn about the school and my new team members at the same time. I was able to share my thoughts too instead of just listening to the veterans.	1. **Assembly Program Orientation**—I got tired of being in the auditorium and listening to all the presenters tell me things I had to go over in the school's handbook. I kept thinking about all I needed to do in my room.
How I felt: Glad to be a member of this team and to feel that my colleagues cared about what I said.	How I felt: Frustrated that I couldn't work on my room and bored and overwhelmed with the way I was receiving information.
To what do I attribute that feeling? The welcoming nature of my team and my need to feel that they respect me and listen to what I say.	To what do I attribute that feeling? I get bored easily and believe I can find out the information I need by reading it in the handbook. I felt like I would run out of time to get my room ready.
How might I change my responses if I do not like them? I would like to be more patient and less nervous about getting things done. I need to be more accepting of other ways of doing things and if I am bored I need to find a way to unobtrusively take care of my own style of learning. I could read the book while presenters are talking.	

Chapter 6

Ten Tips About Similarities and Differences in Decentralized Complex Networks

Collegial partners use both their similarities and their differences to complement each other within complex networks.

Network Architectures

According to Davis and Sumara (2006), in network theory there are three kinds of network architectures: centralized, distributed, and decentralized. (See Figure 6.1, page 104.) Centralized networks are most efficient in terms of making decisions from a global perspective and attempting to establish strong ties to one centralized source (such as the principal or a central office); however, the problem with this kind of network is that if a problem occurs at the center (e.g., if the global perspective is faulty), massive failures can result. Another problem with centralized networks is that they are less robust; they do not try to establish strong ties among the parts of the system that are distant from the center. Therefore, they may not support local parts of the network in their ability to create and implement useful programs and to resolve difficult problems. In contrast, although distributed networks can be more robust and less susceptible to massive failures, efficiency can be lost if not enough members accept responsibility for being fully knowledgeable and accountable for creating and implementing

Figure 6.1 Three Network Architectures

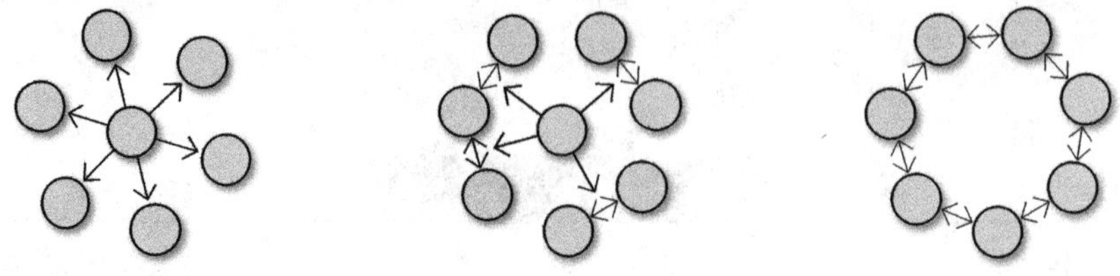

Source: Adapted from Davis and Sumara (2006, p. 52).

programs and solutions to problems. A distributed school network would be highly in favor of establishing learning communities within their school; however, this community might lose efficiency if its members do not fully understand how to work together to create and implement useful programs and resolve difficult problems.

Decentralized networks most closely describe how complex systems function; therefore, school leaders and others might use their knowledge of this kind of network to incorporate the most useful aspects of centralized and distributed networks. For example, because decentralized networks are both efficient and robust, they are highly useful as models for learning communities. In this kind of decentralized system, ideas from a more global or centralized perspective interact with the short-range relationships that create and implement ideas locally. In other words, although the centralized system has weaker ties to the decentralized members of the system, it still can influence the learning community's efficiency. The centralized system also recognizes the value of local systems to create programs and resolve problems.

Describing Decentralized Complex Social Systems Like Mentoring and Coaching

Because complex systems are decentralized, they do not fit well in network architectures that leaders design to be centralized (i.e., hierarchical). Even if decision makers set up their district and schools to rely on a centralized network in which information and resources flow from a district leader or a principal to those who are charged with implementation, because they are dealing with complex systems, their design may not function as they predict or hope it will. In decentralized complex systems, those who use information and resources conceptualized from a global perspective adapt them through their local perspectives in order to make them more efficient and robust for each unique situation.

How Mentors and Novices Handled Centralized Decisions at Lincoln

As mentioned previously, the mentors and coaches at Lincoln often adjusted the decisions from the district and from administrators. The school was struggling with accountability measures, and administrators and teachers experienced many cases in which the district office made decisions that had a tremendous effect on the school. The following two examples show how partnerships adapted centralized decisions to make them useful for their unique setting.

- Central office required that sixty percent of a teacher's students pass the end-of-course test. In order to help those who did not make that goal resist the tendency to give up and shut down, the teachers at Lincoln made a point of valuing the *progress* students made from year to year rather than only valuing the percentage of students passing the test.
- The district office required individual lesson plans for each teacher; however, a mentor/coach convinced the principal that teachers who were all teaching the same scripted lessons should be able to write one lesson plan that was co-constructed and that followed the scripted lesson content.

Tip #1: If decision makers working from a global perspective and those implementing their decisions locally recognize the value of both perspectives, then they may work together to make decisions regarding policies and procedures. It may take a bit longer and could be a messier process, but adding this step could improve the chances that decision makers will implement more useful policies and procedures and that teachers will respect and implement those policies and procedures with fidelity. When the people implementing a policy or procedure help to construct it, then they are more likely to comply with it.

If decision makers do not take the time to gather input from local sources, those at the local level might have complex conversations about how they might be able to adjust the decisions made without their input. Collegial partners who have had experience making these adjustments within their districts could provide valuable insights. In addition, novice and struggling teachers should be honest and open with their colleagues regarding their thoughts and feelings about their abilities to implement those policies and procedures. Having recently come from the typically idealistic world of teacher education, novice teachers may have their own ideas about how district policies and procedures match the current educational research. If mentors, coaches, and novices are able to have honest dialogue about centralized decisions, they could make some useful adjustments.

Decentralizing Collegial Partner Assignments

In many schools it seems necessary to centralize the matching of mentors and coaches with novice and struggling teachers by having a principal or designee make the matches. According to some researchers (e.g., Kram, 1988), formal assignments are less successful in terms of relationship building than allowing mentors and mentees to choose each other. Although it seems ideal to allow mentors and mentees to find each other, realistically it may create problems because some teachers (like novices) need immediate help and often cannot wait to find out if they align well with a mentor/coach.

Flexibility with Matching

At Lincoln, mentors, coaches, and novices exemplified many ways of addressing the assignment issue. Lincoln had someone assigned to oversee the mentoring and coaching program, and that person made the formal assignments. Despite these centralized formal pairings, the teachers at Lincoln made some adjustments:

- One novice had a formally assigned mentor, but because he had been the practice teacher of the curriculum coach, he considered her to be his *real mentor*.
- Another novice had an assigned mentor, but because he did not have much in common with this mentor, he asked the department chair, who was already mentoring another novice, to be his informal mentor.
- Another novice teacher had a formally assigned mentor/coach; however, even though she had a wonderful relationship with her mentor, she also received mentoring from a team member who was not a mentor but who had been teaching longer and who also had ideas in common with the novice.
- The mentor coordinator assigned a part-time content coach to mentor a novice teacher; however, because this content coach/mentor was only in the building two days per week and had many other responsibilities, the novice asked a second-year teacher to mentor her.

Tip #2: After initial matching, centralized decision makers may be able to share subsequent decisions about matching collegial partners. For example, even if someone makes initial assignments, school leaders might encourage mentors and novices to establish their own relationships. As I suggested in Chapter 2, school leaders may consider stating at the beginning of the school year that assignments are "temporary" until partnerships agree that they should continue to identify their relationships as partnerships. School leaders may consider informing partners that these pairings will last for three weeks to one month, and that at the end of that period, these partnerships could make their own arrangements for either formalizing their partnership status or informing school leaders that they have formed other partnerships.

School leaders can set the tone for these adjusted relationships by doing the following:

- being very clear that temporary relationships are just to get teachers started, but that mentors/coaches and novices/struggling teachers should establish their own permanent relationships
- stating that if partners do not change their temporary status to permanent, no one should assume that either party was deficient
- encouraging partnerships to keep their rationales for changing their relationships confidential
- cautioning partners against only choosing those most like themselves; growth often comes from less comfortable relationships

Scale-Free Networks

Scale-free networks change their own structures in order to adapt and thrive. Researchers can measure these structures; however, traditional statistical procedures that rely on the bell curve are not useful to measure them. Scale-free networks rely instead on power statistics because the determination of significance does not congregate around averages. Instead, many small events or one large event can be important to describe phenomena. For example, one important event in the life of a teacher can be highly important in terms of his or her practices or decisions. Figure 6.2 on page 108 graphically depicts these concepts.

Figure 6.2 Scale-Free Networks

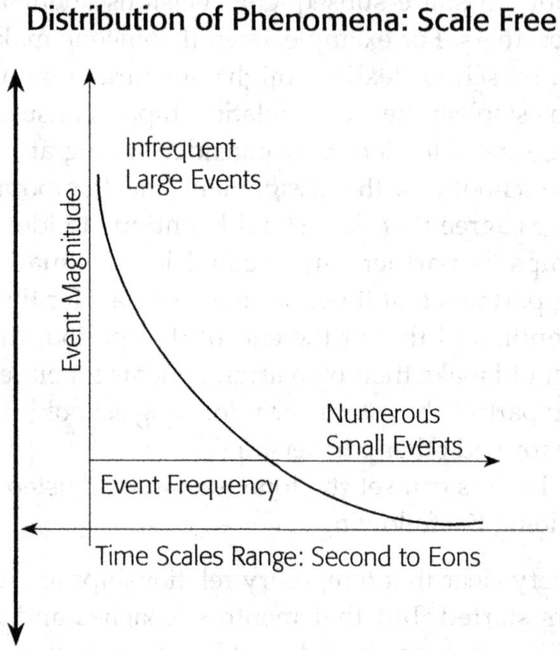

Source: Reproduced from Waterman (2012, p. 262).

"I Almost Quit"

A story from one of the teachers at Lincoln provides an excellent example of how one powerful event was significant in terms of the retention of a valuable teacher.

> During first semester, Mr. Cook "got behind in [his] paperwork." He did not have his "PEPs [Personalized Educations Plans] finished" and he "was falling behind in grading [his] work." Mr. Cook also worked a second job, so that was part of the issue. He just could not "manage" it all. It was "too much stress." He decided to quit teaching.
>
> Mr. Cook typed his "letter of resignation," and he was ready to go turn it in, but Mrs. Herman, his mentor, had helped him get the job, so he decided it would not be respectful of him to "just walk out." He decided to tell her what he planned to do. He said to Mrs. Herman, "I'm quitting."
>
> Mrs. Herman said, "You're going to do what?"...

> Mrs. Herman and Mr. Cook had a "heart to heart for maybe thirty minutes." That talk was on a Thursday. He came back on Friday and he "took the weekend to think it over." Mr. Cook decided, "I'm going to give it one more shot." (Waterman, 2012, pp. 304–306)

It could be an exaggeration that one person actually prevented another from quitting the profession; however, it is undeniable that Mrs. Herman's relationship with Mr. Cook seemed to play an important role in his decision to remain in the profession. One can never underestimate the power of a single conversation to influence big decisions.

Tip #3: Decision makers might accept that scale-free power statistics supply the most useful research-based evidence regarding complex systems such as those between collegial partners. This means that attempting to use scale-based (i.e., bell curve) and inferential statistics to predict how partnerships will behave can be less useful and can even create false assumptions. Educators might use descriptive statistics to organize and describe quantifiable data, such as how often a mentor and novice met or how many teachers left the school. The problem occurs when educators attempt to do these two things: (1) infer that one event or set of events caused or correlated with another event or set of events (e.g., certain school conflicts caused teachers to leave) or (2) assume that the discovery of behavior patterns indicates a rationale for implementing a program that will address everyone's needs (e.g., requiring novices to meet with their mentors once per week because statistics show that novices who meet with mentors at least once per week are more likely to stay in the profession). In the national atmosphere of accountability and the insistence on empirical evidence, educators might carefully evaluate their use of scale-based and inferential evidence-based research to support policies that address complex systems like mentoring and coaching. They might use instead the discovery of actions that appear to be important regardless of their frequency. "The Starfish Story" suggests that although the act of throwing individual starfish back into the sea may not have been important to those remaining on the beach, it *was* important to the ones that were thrown back (Eisely, 1969). Qualitative studies that include teachers' stories, such as the one Mr. Cook told, can be useful data that stakeholders might consider when they make decisions.

Structure-Determined Systems

Complex systems are not only scale-free but also structure-determined. This means, according to Davis and Sumara (2006), that the system itself, not the context in which it is functioning, decides how it will change. A structure-determined nature demonstrates that the concepts of cause and effect are irrelevant for describing complex systems. Cause and effect are useful concepts for describing what happens in simple and complicated systems, not complex ones. For example, the toy dancer metaphor shows that someone outside the dancers decides how they will dance—that is, the person who created the dancers and the person who opens the box or pushes the buttons that cause them to dance. The outside force causes a certain response from the simple or complicated system. This is not true for complex systems. In a complex system, no matter what an outside source does, the dancers determine for themselves how they will respond.

> **Tip #4:** It can be important to collect and organize data using descriptive statistics; however, educators might keep in mind that complex systems are structure-determined, so that outside forces do not control them. If educators acknowledge that program planning is subject to surprising responses from those who implement it, they may design programs that *plan for complexity*. In other words, they might suggest initiatives that are flexible enough to include a variety of responses. Decision makers who plan for complexity might strongly suggest that school leaders provide mentors for novices, but they would avoid placing strict requirements on how those mentors and novices organize their relationships. They might also ask mentors and novices to create some kind of record of their work together, but they would avoid requiring a specific type of evidence.

Learning Through Redundancy and Diversity

The way the structure-determined, complex system learns has a great deal to do with two additional concepts: redundancy and diversity. Internal redundancy (similarities and commonalities) includes the strong ties between elements of the system that facilitate communication and comfort among those elements. For example, people usually need to have some common ground on which to establish their relationships. Without some redundancy, it could be nearly impossible for collegial partners to work together. On the other side is the concept of internal diversity (differences), which includes the weak ties between elements of the system that facilitate challenge and movement (growth and change) away from comfort and the status quo. In partnerships there usually are more instances of redundancy than diversity. If there is too much redundancy and not enough diversity, however, the system could stagnate and cease to have meaning. On the other hand, if there is not enough redundancy and too much diversity, the system could fall apart from lack of attachment.

Redundancy (Similarities)

At Lincoln, mentors/coaches and novices expressed internal redundancy through sharing similar teaching philosophies and goals, teaching the same content and students with similar developmental levels, and seeing themselves as special people who understood how to work with their special population (see Figure 6.3).

Figure 6.3 Redundancies (Similarities)

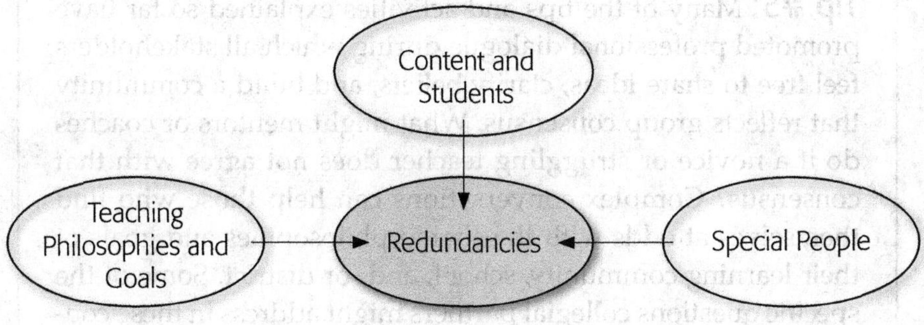

Teaching Philosophies and Goals

Teachers who share similar philosophies and common goals are usually able to talk comfortably about how to handle topics such as classroom discipline, lesson planning, and student accountability. Even if they disagree about procedure, they can at least begin a conversation that includes some common assumptions. When teachers have similar philosophies and common goals, they are much more likely to be able to work through the times when they may have some disagreement about how to approach specific challenges. Sharing teaching philosophies and common goals can provide a strong basis from which teachers may try new ideas. Most important, philosophically-aligned teachers can convey a sense of unity within the school culture, thus having a positive effect on student morale.

Shared Philosophies and Common Goals at Lincoln

Most of the mentors/coaches and novices at Lincoln had similar philosophies and common teaching goals, which made it easier for them to work together and helped them survive occasions when they felt under considerable pressure from forces outside of their school culture. Shared philosophies included unconditionally caring for their students, handling student disruptions on their own, accepting that test scores are evidence of student learning and teachers' skills, and counting on strong student–teacher relationships to facilitate the learning process. Most of my research participants seemed aligned regarding these philosophies; nevertheless, it was apparent when any one of them seemed to have a different view. For example, rather than believing that it was the duty of teachers to handle their own discipline problems, Mrs. Baker believed that in many cases it was the responsibility of administrators to discipline so that she could teach. This divergence from the dominant school philosophy may have contributed to her job loss at the end of the year.

> **Tip #5:** Many of the tips and activities explained so far have promoted professional dialogue during which all stakeholders feel free to share ideas, clarify beliefs, and build a community that reflects group consensus. What might mentors or coaches do if a novice or struggling teacher does not agree with that consensus? Complex conversations can help those who find themselves at odds with the shared philosophies and goals of their learning community, school, and/or district. Some of the specific questions collegial partners might address in these conversations are as follows:
>
> - In what areas do you sense that your teaching philosophies do not align with the dominant philosophies of our school?
> - If you sense a difference, how do you plan to stay true to your teaching philosophies and goals if you continue to teach at this school?
> - What steps might you take to re-evaluate your philosophies in light of their differences with the school culture in which you are working?
> - If you feel a need to adjust your deeply-held philosophies, how might that affect your teaching?
> - How might adjusting your deeply-held philosophies about teaching affect your relationships with others in the school?

Content and Students

It seems logical that teachers who teach similar content and similar students could find it easier to work together in collegial partnerships. For example, they may find it easier to pool their ideas in order to save time and energy. Having the same kinds of content could maximize the possibility that partners could be able to help each other determine how to adjust lessons for various learners, where to find interesting enrichment or remedial materials, and what kinds of lesson models work best to teach certain content objectives. They may also be able to empathize more easily with each other because they could have similar challenges with their students.

Teaching Similar Students and Content at Lincoln

One of the most striking examples of the benefits of teachers teaching similar content and students occurred in the case of Mrs. Stewart. She and three other teachers taught the same specialized curriculum, designed especially for struggling students. Their coach, Mrs. Herman, was able to help these four teachers construct a collaborative lesson plan for each learning goal. Interestingly, Mrs. Stewart was able to determine that if the lesson worked for her colleague Mrs. Anderson, it would also work for her, and if it did not work for Mrs. Anderson it would not work for her. Having the same curriculum materials, the same scripted lessons, and the same challenging student population provided the basis for a great deal of peer mentoring and coaching.

Tip #6: Learning communities can resolve many of the problems school leaders encounter when they are trying to match mentors or coaches with novices or struggling teachers according to their subjects/grade levels and the developmental levels of their students. It simply may not work for novices or struggling teachers to have collegial partners who align with them perfectly. For example, some struggling schools may not have enough partners to work with an abundance of novices and struggling/teachers. In these cases, temporary pairing could provide initial help, but then for specific content collaboration and student–teacher relationship problem solving, novices and struggling teachers might find their own matches. When novices and struggling teachers understand and accept that they share the responsibility of finding their own helping relationships, school leaders can rest assured that their faculty have instituted or are working on instituting a "culture of helping."

Special People

Seeing their school and themselves as special has the potential to unify faculty for the purposes of collaboration and the development of a culture of helping. When a group of people concur that they share special skills and talents that help them address their school's special needs, they stand a better chance of being able to work together. The concept of what it means to qualify as a "special person" can align throughout an entire school or it can be different among departments. For example, the math department or the third grade may have a strong notion of what it means to be a special math teacher or a special third-grade teacher. Unfortunately, this view can serve the purpose of excluding those who do not seem to fit the dominant notion of what it means to be "special person" in the school. If a new person coming into a school does not understand what it means to be a "special person," he or she may not have a chance to learn how to qualify.

Two "Knuckleheads"

The mentors/coaches and novices at Lincoln said often that it took a special teacher to make it at their school. Some of those who did not qualify to teach at Lincoln were those with too much education (e.g., Ph.Ds). The rationale for rejecting those with too much education was that they found it difficult to interact on the same levels as their students. Other mismatches were those who seemed to lack the patience to form relationships with their students because their expectations for certain kinds of behavior and academic achievement were not realistic. The teachers who had struggled in school themselves were often the ones who found it easiest to relate to the students. For example, Mrs. Rankin (mentor) and Ms. Captain (novice) agreed that they recognized each other from the beginning as "two knuckleheads" with whom their students could identify and for whom students tended to behave themselves and try to do their school work.

> **Tip #7:** It is important for collegial partners to know that they are special people. School leaders should do their best to nurture that belief so that partners have the potential to connect on a deep level around that special status. Some ideas for nurturing a "special person" designation include the following:
>
> - having regular celebrations that acknowledge special individuals, special teams, and special partners
> - developing items (t-shirts, water bottles, visors, etc.) that convey a message about the special nature of the school or its vision

- ♦ having a meeting toward the beginning of the year during which the school makes clear its underlying assumptions about what makes a teacher a special person. Include in that meeting discussion about why a teacher may want to consider these values to determine if they match their school. (See activities in Chapter 1 about determining if someone is a good match for the school.)
- ♦ finding ways to explore teachers' feelings when they do not feel accepted into the "special person" category. Exploring these feelings in a safe environment with a mentor/coach can help novices/struggling teachers learn to cope with their feelings of not belonging.

Diversity (Differences)

At Lincoln, mentors/coaches and novices expressed internal diversity through their physical characteristics, funds of knowledge, and teaching skills (see Figure 6.4).

Figure 6.4 Diversity (Differences)

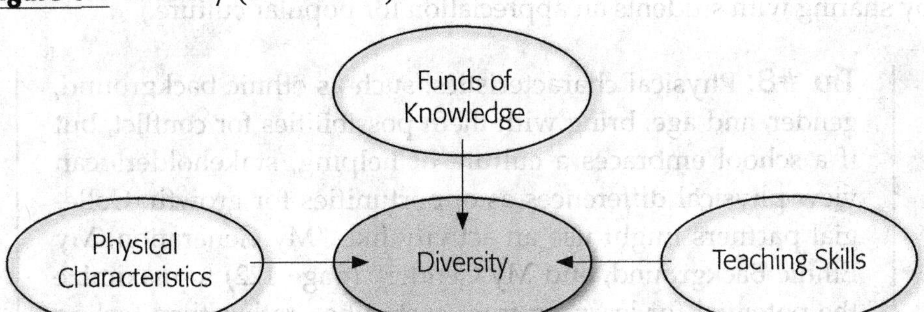

Physical Characteristics

A common physical difference among collegial partners is age because new teachers are usually younger than veteran teachers. In some cases, being from different generations can create conflict, but it can also create opportunities for learning if each generation respects the perspective of the other. Another physical characteristic that can either create conflict or provide opportunities for growth is gender difference. Matching a male with a female in a partnership has the potential for many dilemmas. One of these is sexual attraction, mutual or one-sided. Additionally, paternalism or stereotyping could occur if the mentor/coach is male and the novice or struggling teacher is female. If the mentor or coach is a woman and the novice or struggling teacher is a male, the woman could develop a maternal relationship in which she feels she has to nurture the male instead of respecting his capacity to handle problems without being "mothered." Another personal difference is ethnic background, which presents possible cultural misunderstandings; on the other hand, these differences can also help expand perspectives and help teachers learn how to respect others.

"The Grandmother Respect"

None of the mentor/coach and novice relationships at Lincoln were homogeneous (same ethnic background, same age, or same gender). One of the most interesting pairings was between Mrs. Herman, who had been teaching for over thirty years, and Mr. Cook, who was only a few years older than his students and in his first year of teaching. Mrs. Herman believed that Mr. Cook was one of the most creative and intelligent teachers she had ever worked with, and Mr. Cook said Mrs. Herman was a great role model for him. Mr. Cook did, however, notice a major difference between him and Mrs. Herman. For example, Mr. Cook believed that Mrs. Herman was able to get what he called "the grandmother respect," which he was not entitled to receive. Instead, Mr. Cook found a way to get a different kind of respect by sharing with students an appreciation for popular culture.

> Tip #8: Physical characteristics, such as ethnic background, gender, and age, bring with them possibilities for conflict, but if a school embraces a culture of helping, stakeholders can view physical differences as opportunities for growth. Collegial partners might use an activity like "My Generation, My Ethnic Background, and My Gender" (page 122) to maximize the potential for learning from each other, rather than feeling disconnected or in conflict with each other.

Funds of Knowledge

Differences between collegial partners in terms of their funds of knowledge help them fill gaps for each other. For example, since mentors and coaches are usually veteran teachers, they tend to have knowledge of school culture that exceeds that of novices and struggling teachers. This superior knowledge often helps novices and struggling teachers fill gaps in understanding how to respond to school culture. For example, the mentor or coach may understand and be able to communicate to novices or struggling teachers what it means when a principal or department chair asks for certain kinds of responses. For example, although a school leader may say one thing, he or she might in fact mean something else. Partners might be able to warn novices and struggling teachers to pay attention to actions more than words. They may also explain how much latitude they might have in implementing a school policy. On the other hand, novices might fill in the gaps for veterans because they have just come from "the academy" where they most likely experienced the most up-to-date teaching practices, which can include using new technologies.

Great "Composite Teacher"

Mrs. Stewart's relationship with her informal mentor, Mrs. Anderson, provides an excellent example of the ways collegial partners at Lincoln filled gaps for each other based on their funds of knowledge. According to Mrs. Stewart, she and Mrs. Anderson made a great "composite teacher."

> They made a great composite teacher because Mrs. Stewart was good at "thinking of things" and Mrs. Anderson was "really good at making them concrete." It was reassuring to Mrs. Stewart to know that what would fly in her class would fly in Mrs. Anderson's class and what would sink in her class would also sink in Mrs. Anderson's. (Waterman, 2012, p. 294)

Mrs. Rankin (mentor) and Ms. Captain (novice) also filled gaps for each other, mainly because Mrs. Rankin helped Ms. Captain understand how to work with challenging students, and Ms. Captain helped Mrs. Rankin learn how to use technology to teach content information that was relatively new since Mrs. Rankin had been in college. Also, regarding funds of knowledge, I was most concerned that I often heard veteran mentors/coaches complain about those who seemed too smart for their school. For example, according to Mrs. Stanley (mentor), school leaders never gave Mrs. Lawson (novice), one of the brightest teachers in her department, a chance to teach advanced placement students. Several teachers in the department believed that both Mrs. Lawson and the advanced placement students might have experienced an excellent connection.

> **Tip #9:** In a culture of helping, both veterans and novices or those who struggle have a strong sense of respect for various kinds of knowledge. School leaders and collegial partners might use an activity like "K-W-L" in order to learn about each other for the purpose of filling gaps. School leaders can model respect for the fund of knowledge that each person brings to

the school. Leaders might use an activity like "Our Funds of Knowledge and Skills" (page 123) to demonstrate their belief in the collective power of sharing knowledge among professionals. They can support those teachers who have superior funds of knowledge, but who may have difficulty relating to students. If leaders see exceptionally bright teachers as assets rather than deficiencies, they may consider giving these bright people time to learn to connect with their students. Even though they might believe that superior knowledge does not make someone a great teacher, they might also believe that even bright people need time to gain new knowledge.

Teaching Skills

Diversity in teaching skills is another important way that collegial partners fill gaps for each other. Mentors and coaches have developed excellent pedagogical skills that can be useful for novices and struggling teachers to learn, but experienced teachers might also learn some skills from novices and struggling teachers. Even if teachers are new to the classroom or are struggling with certain aspects of teaching, it is important that mentors and coaches discover the skills these new or struggling teachers might bring to the school.

Some Skills Were Better Than Others

The mentors/coaches at Lincoln often acknowledged that novices had some skills superior to theirs. For example, although Mr. Manzetti (mentor) was concerned that Mrs. Baker (novice) struggled with classroom management, he determined that her approaches to some aspects of the curriculum were superior to his. Also of interest was Mrs. Truitt (mentor), one of the strongest teachers at the school, who concluded that when it came to teaching advanced students, Mr. Hansen's (novice) laid-back and quiet teaching style was superior to her more aggressive style. Finally, although Mrs. Stanley was not enthusiastic about Mrs. Lawson's teacher presence, she believed that her ability to break things down for students was exceptional. These are just a few examples of the exceptional skills demonstrated by novices/struggling teachers at Lincoln. They demonstrate that although novices/struggling teachers may have weaknesses in some pedagogical areas, they also have strengths.

Tip #10: Having an appreciative versus a deficit perspective can promote a culture of helping in which all stakeholders can feel they have skills to offer the school (Cooperrider et al., 2007; Gold, 1996). School leaders and collegial partners might establish this perspective by first making a commitment to appreciation versus deficiency, and then practicing that commitment until they thoroughly incorporate it within their rhetoric and their decisions. Finally, school leaders and partners hold each other accountable for challenging any deficit thinking. They might do this through authentic dialogue during which they challenge the use of language that conveys a deficit perspective. If novice or struggling teachers are having difficulty meeting expectations, school leaders and partners might talk about how they can help these teachers get what they need to fulfill their those expectations rather than focusing on how they are not meeting them. By promoting a positive perspective, observations and evaluations become opportunities for improvement rather than threats to job security.

Activities

Clarifying Our Beliefs

This activity might be useful for a faculty meeting, in a learning community, or with collegial partnerships. Note that for the sake of brevity, I am collapsing the notions of beliefs, philosophies, and values into one category called "beliefs." There are differences among these three terms, but for the purposes of this exercise, I think it works to call them all beliefs. Feel free to differentiate them if you feel that is important. Participants will need paper, pencils, a flip chart, an easel, and markers.

Step 1: The person leading the session acknowledges the following:

- There are some beliefs, philosophies, and values that the majority of the teachers and administrators seem to share at this school.
- Those common beliefs, etc. are not always captured in our vision, mission, and values statements (if the school has those kinds of statements).
- For newcomers and for veterans, it would be useful to clearly state those common beliefs.
- We need to determine some procedures for evaluating our beliefs and practices on a regular basis throughout the year, not just at the beginning.

Step 2: If it is a large group, get into groups of five to eight to brainstorm a list of "Our Common Beliefs." A volunteer might record these answers on a flip chart that has written at the top of the first page, "The people who work at this school believe that … (every child has the potential for success, teachers should handle their own discipline problems, etc.)."

Step 3: Have a conversation in which members of the group suggest combining any of the ideas because they are similar.

Step 4: After the list has been refined into a list of beliefs that are each distinctly different from each other, consider prioritizing that list (although that is not necessary). If you broke into smaller groups, ask a volunteer to share the list with the larger group and construct a whole-group list.

Step 5: Have a candid conversation (break into smaller groups if you are using this as a whole-faculty exercise) that answers these questions:

- How might we evaluate our beliefs in terms of educational research?
- How might we evaluate our beliefs in terms of our practices?
- What happens to those whose behaviors and words do not align with these common beliefs?

- If we believe we should adjust our beliefs or make room for dissenting beliefs, how would we do that?
- How do we plan to check out our fidelity to our beliefs throughout the school year?

Step 6: Record the list and the answers to the questions. Publish the information in some manner (for example, send everyone an email attachment with the information).

Special People

Faculties might celebrate their "special person" status. Here are some ideas in addition to the usual faculty holiday parties, teacher appreciation week, faculty of the month and year contests, PTA recognitions, or other traditional ways faculty and staff show appreciation for each other.

- Have a "Special Person Event" at least once per quarter. During this event, which should occur away from the school, provide food and drink (or access to them if you cannot afford it in your budget). During this event, hold a "Special Person Toasting Contest." Tell members of the faculty that you are going to have a contest to see who can make the most "over-the-top" toast to honor a fellow faculty member. Give prizes, ribbons, or funny trophies for the best ones.
- Once per quarter or at least twice per year, a committee representing each department should create "Thank You for Being a Special Person" notes for each person on staff, the more personal the better.
- Once per quarter or at least twice per year, designated faculty should collaborate to conduct a "Thank You for Being Special" note-writing initiative among the student body. Students could write notes thanking their homeroom teachers (for secondary) or their teachers for elementary. Make sure that every teacher gets a note, if possible.
- At least once per quarter or twice per year, teachers should help students thank other members of the staff, such as principals, counselors, librarians, cafeteria staff, security associates, janitors, or anyone else who works at the school.
- Counselors or a team of teachers might organize a year-long "Secret Admirer" initiative in which they match members of the faculty and staff who want to participate. Those who participate agree to show appreciation for their assigned person at least once per month. Organizers might determine a specific day for sharing appreciation or just suggest it happen once per month.
- Make buttons that say something like "VIT" (Very Important Teacher) and include the school's logo, mascot, motto, or slogan. Principals might hand these out after they observe a teacher or for special recognition during faculty meetings.

My Generation, My Ethnic Background, and My Gender

Large groups, a learning community, or partners might use this activity to better understand the role diversity could play in their relationships.

Step 1: Give each participant a copy of the chart below.

Step 2: Participants answer the questions on the side of the chart that refers to them (mentor/coach or novice/teacher).

Step 3: Participants take turns interviewing each other to fill out the other side of the chart.

Step 4: Participants separate to complete the boxes under each category (age, ethnic background, gender) that asks them to list what their differences or similarities for each category might teach them. For example, "What can I learn from our differences or similarities in ethnic background?"

Step 5: Participants take turns sharing what they put in each of these boxes.

Assessing Our Physical Differences or Similarities

<table>
<tr><th></th><th>Mentor/Coach</th><th>Novice/Teacher</th></tr>
<tr><td rowspan="2">Age</td><td>How does my age affect my teaching?</td><td>How does my age affect my teaching?</td></tr>
<tr><td colspan="2">What can I learn from our differences or similarities in age?</td></tr>
<tr><td rowspan="2">Ethnic Background</td><td>How does my ethnic background affect my teaching?</td><td>How does my ethnic background affect my teaching?</td></tr>
<tr><td colspan="2">What can I learn from our differences or similarities in ethnic background?</td></tr>
<tr><td rowspan="2">Gender</td><td>How does my gender affect my teaching?</td><td>How does my gender affect my teaching?</td></tr>
<tr><td colspan="2">What can I learn from our differences or similarities in gender?</td></tr>
</table>

K-W-L for Helpers

This activity, which teachers use as an instructional technique, can also help collegial partners develop an understanding of the knowledge and skills they each bring to their schools. Whole faculties, learning communities, or partners might use this activity.

Step 1: Participants choose a topic that is relevant to their grade-level teaching objectives.

Step 2: They use the template below to brainstorm a list of what they already know about the topic. This brainstorming can be individual or collaborative.

Step 3: Participants determine what they would like to know about the topic that would enrich their ability to teach their objectives.

Step 4: Participants decide how they will learn about the topic. For example, they might agree to share the responsibility for researching a specific aspect of the topic.

Know	Want to Know	How to Learn

Our Funds of Knowledge and Skills

School leaders may want to determine the kinds of knowledge and skills individual teachers at their school have, and they may also want to access the total fund of knowledge and skills that exist in their school. This can be a source of pride and foster the potential for collaboration. School leaders might develop a survey that helps them assess some general categories such as the following:

Directions: Circle the S for each statement that describes you.

Pedagogy	
S1	I know how to write essential questions and learning objectives.
S2	I know how to differentiate instruction using multiple intelligences.
S3	I know how to differentiate instruction using learning styles.
S4	I know how to use concept mapping.
S5	I know how to use cooperative learning.
Classroom Management	
S1	I know how to lead a classroom meeting.
S2	I know how to use logical consequences as a way of managing student behavior.
S3	I know how to collaborate with students to make a list of class rules.
S4	I know how to develop relationships with my students so that they respect me.
S5	I know how to partner with parents to help support my discipline plans.

(continued)

Content Knowledge	
S1	I have a thorough knowledge of the learning objectives for my subject area.
S2	I have been teaching my subject for ______ years, and I have a thorough understanding of my subject/grade level.
S3	I have taken several courses and/or continuing education courses in my subject, and I feel I have extensive knowledge of my subject/grade level.

After teachers have completed the survey, school leaders can complete a profile for each teacher and can count up totals to determine a composite for the school. For example, school leaders might construct charts such as the following to describe the funds of knowledge and skills at their school.

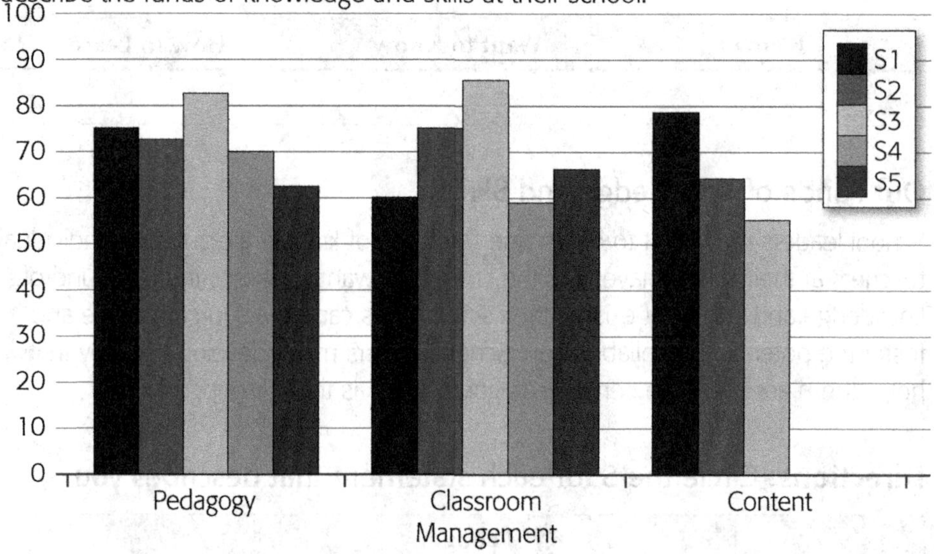

Do We Appreciate Each Other?

School leaders may consider using a survey to find out how well faculty and staff appreciate each other at their school. Faculty and staff may complete the survey anonymously or by identifying themselves. The findings can become a great topic for discussion that includes planning to improve or to maintain the current levels of appreciation.

Appreciation Survey

Circle the statement that best describes your feelings.			
1. The faculty and staff at this school make a point of saying positive things about each other.			
Strongly Disagree	Disagree	Agree	Strongly Agree
2. The faculty and staff at this school are rarely critical of one another.			
Strongly Disagree	Disagree	Agree	Strongly Agree
3. I feel appreciated at this school.			
Strongly Disagree	Disagree	Agree	Strongly Agree
4. School leaders often make positive statements about faculty and staff at our school.			
Strongly Disagree	Disagree	Agree	Strongly Agree
5. Our school makes a point of avoiding deficit thinking (e.g., critical and negative thinking).			
Strongly Disagree	Disagree	Agree	Strongly Agree

Chapter 7

Eight Tips for Capacity Building

Collegial partnerships build the personal capacity of those involved and the collective capacity of staff and faculty to handle school challenges.

Ecologically Based Sustainable Capacity Building

According to Mitchell and Sackney (2001, 2009), people can work together to build sustainable learning communities especially if they understand and implement certain complex ecological concepts. What follows is an explanation of each of these concepts and how they might apply to the capacity-building nature of mentor/coach and novice/struggling teacher relationships. Mitchell and Sackney proposed that the following ideas support ecologically based capacity building: collegial dynamics, collaborative cultures, and shared understandings. I added synchronicity (Jaworski, 1996; Jung, 1960) and the Theory of the U. Within collegial dynamics, I included ideas about sponsorship and protection (Kram, 1988), which come from another philosophical tradition but which I felt were important to describe, and authentic professional dialogue, which included acknowledgement, advocacy, inquiry, and invitation. (See Figure 7.1, page 128.)

Figure 7.1 Elements of Ecologically Based Sustainable Capacity Building

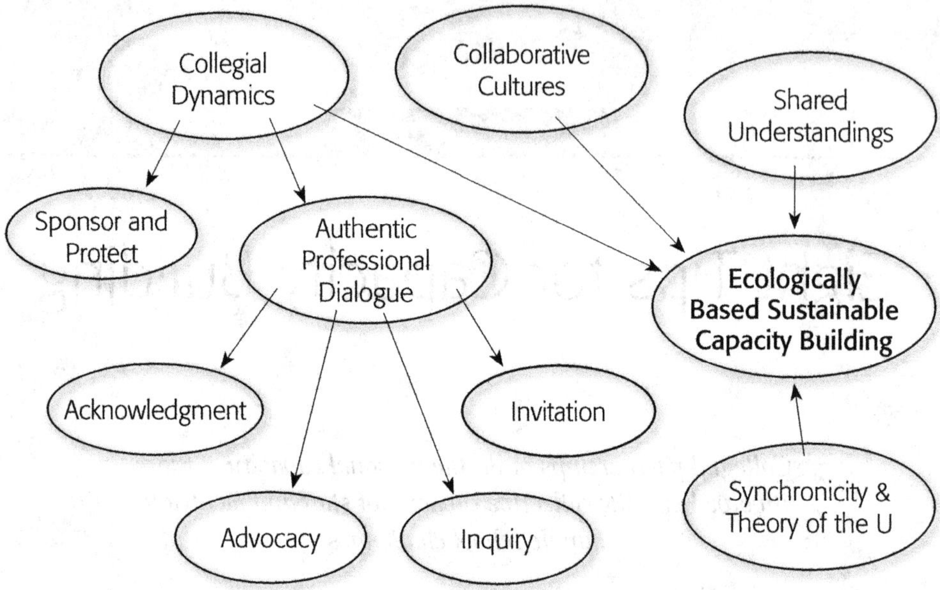

A Note About Sustainability

Teaching practices, policies, and procedures that resonate most closely with the needs and styles of those using them stand the best chance of sustainability. For example, instituting a journaling initiative to help novices and struggling teachers reflect on their practices might be an excellent strategy for the English department but may not work at all in the Math department. We can forget sometimes that practices, policies, and procedures that seem logical to us in terms of sustainability may not last very long for others. Those practices and procedures that are not sustainable tend to frustrate educators. For example, teachers and administrators often state that the proposed new ideas sound a lot like those they used three years ago but with new jargon. Decision makers might avoid frustrating those implementing their proposed practices, policies, and procedures by carefully considering the sustainability possibilities for *all* stakeholders affected by their decisions.

Collegial Dynamics

Collegial dynamics as described by Mitchell and Sackney (2001, 2009) are those processes or motivational forces that describe how groups of people work together. Useful collegial dynamics help people handle conflicts that could destroy their ability to work as a unified group. Several kinds of collegial dynamics are relevant to mentoring and coaching, and even though most of those I explored reflected the work of Mitchell and Sackney, I also noted two processes (sponsorship and protection) that do not align with their conceptualization of ecological capacity building (Mitchell & Sackney, 2001, 2009). Unfortunately, they were processes I observed at Lincoln. Although my research participants used these processes, they are not optimal when one is trying to sustain capacity-building collegial dynamics.

Sponsorship typically occurs when mentors or coaches use their personal relationships within the school to help novices or struggling teachers also develop those relationships. For example, mentors and coaches who have excellent relationships with their principals because they have demonstrated that they are trustworthy and skilled professionals might vouch for the trustworthiness and skills of novices and struggling teachers. By vouching for their colleagues, they lend their support to help novices and struggling teachers develop a positive reputation in the school and with the leadership.

Unfortunately, even though school leaders most often trust mentors and coaches, they do not trust all of them. In addition, it can be risky for mentors and coaches to promote novices and struggling teachers to school leaders because even though a collegial partner might be imparting positive information, it is still information that demonstrates a power differential, could be evaluative, and could break confidentiality.

Sponsorship: "I Just See a … Teacher!"

A story from Mrs. Stewart provides an excellent example of how her mentor/coach, Mrs. Herman, sponsored her.

> One day after Dr. Thomas (pseudonym), the principal, observed Mrs. Stewart, he said, "What do you think about having Mrs. Herman as your mentor?" Mrs. Stewart answered, "Oh, she's great!" And Dr. Thomas replied, "She said when she looks at you, she just *sees* a … teacher. She just *sees* one." Mrs. Herman had never said that to Mrs. Stewart and hearing this praise by way of Dr. Thomas meant more to her and was more powerful than telling her directly. It was more meaningful for her "to be putting *my* reputation out like that" because at Lincoln "rep matter[ed]" and "it [was] sink or swim as far as your reputation." Mrs. Stewart realized that when someone like Mrs. Herman, who had 30 years of experience as a … teacher, said she was "on point," that carried a great deal of weight with the principal and with others in the school. (Waterman, 2012, p. 321)

Mentors/coaches sponsored novices with administrators, and other novices and novices sponsored each other in their relationships with students and parents. For example, Mr. Cook used his relationship with a student and her parents to help Mrs. Baker. He told Mrs. Baker, who was having problems establishing a working relationship with the student and her parents, that he would use his good relationship with them to help her. He told his student and her parents that if the student did not treat Mrs. Baker with respect that he would help Mrs. Baker address the problem with the student's parents.

> **Tip #1:** Although it is typical in traditional mentoring relationships, sponsorship can create some confusing dynamics. If collegial partners feel they need to sponsor their novice or struggling teachers, they may avoid sounding evaluative and breaking confidentiality if they consider being specific about the behavior they are promoting and asking for permission to mention that specific behavior to a specific person. For example, mentors/coaches might say something like this: "Would you like for me to let the principal know that you are skilled at integrating learning styles inventories with the objectives listed in our curriculum guide?" Note that I mentioned a specific person (the principal) and that I used no evaluative words such as "you have an exceptional ability" or "you are highly talented in your ability."

Protection

Another collegial dynamic that collegial partners traditionally have used on behalf of novices and struggling teachers is protection, which is even more difficult to provide than sponsorship. Protection assumes that someone is a victim and that someone else might be able to save him or her. The kinds of useful protection mentors/coaches might provide for novices/struggling teachers seem limited, but nevertheless they may occur. For example, some teachers can feel that without some protection from the conflicts that often occur in schools, they are left to "sink." In order to address this sinking sensation, partnerships may perceive that mentors and coaches can provide protective support until novices or struggling teachers can start swimming on their own. In adversarial school environments, novices and struggling teachers may need protection; however, if conflict is excessive and partners feel they constantly need to protect novices and struggling teachers, there could be something the school needs to take steps to address. In addition, based on my findings, it seems that mentors and coaches cannot protect novices and struggling teachers from losing their teaching positions. Protection within a school system seems limited to providing a kind of scaffolding service rather than a sheltering one, and partners need to be extremely careful that they stay neutral in terms of aligning themselves with novices and struggling teachers against administrators, students, parents, or colleagues. In other words, partnerships need to understand the concept of triangulation.

Triangulation

Protecting someone can be extremely difficult, and falling into the trap of siding with someone who comes into conflict with someone else can be unhealthy. Systems theorist and psychologist Murray Bowen (1978) proposed a theory of the triangle to describe how, in times of stress, one member of a two-person relationship (i.e., a dyad) may go to a third, less-involved person to create a coalition to strengthen his or her stance against the other member of the dyad; this is primary triangulation. In addition, the triangle may bring in a fourth person to help balance the conflict; this is secondary triangulation. The member of the dyad who is least comfortable brings in one or more others to help him or her escape the tension. According to Bowen (1978), in a helping relationship, the helper should remain *neutral* regarding emotional issues that might occur between two people or among three or more. By avoiding an emotional response to the situation, mentors/coaches may be able to avoid triangulation.

The process of triangulation has implications for the development of conflicts between mentors/coaches and novices/struggling teachers and their students, principals, parents and other colleagues. For example, when school polices do not allow teachers to deal directly with student misbehavior, a conflict between a teacher and student can become a dysfunctional triangle when one of them involves someone else, such as a principal or mentor/coach (Ingersoll, 2002). In this relationship one member of the triangle may suffer increased anxiety and lower self-esteem. If a collegial partner becomes involved, he or she may have to deal with the dysfunction involved in secondary triangulation. For example, the teacher may call on the mentor or coach to take his or her side against a student, administrator, parent, or colleague. The manner in which the partner handles triangulation can have a significant effect on his or her ability to help the novice or struggling teacher with conflicts.

Protecting: "My First Line of Defense" and "Having Your Back"

Mrs. Baker relied heavily on her mentor, Mr. Manzetti. An excerpt from her story "Diapering, Powdering, and Taking Care" shows how she felt about his role as her mentor.

> Of all those who helped Mrs. Baker, she considered Mr. Manzetti to be her "first line of defense." He was the "first person" she went to when she had a question or needed to know which person she needed to ask to handle something. (Waterman, 2012, p. 307)

Mr. Hansen also felt a sense of protection from his mentor, Mrs. Truitt. He said that she helped him deal with school leaders so that he did not feel intimidated by them, and in many cases she protected him from the stress involved in teaching at a school that the district considered to be low performing. Mr. Hansen's story "On the Bus" shows how he viewed his mentor:

> It was important to Mr. Hansen that he knew Mrs. Truitt had "his back" not just with his "classes but also with administration and everything else." (Waterman, 2012, p. 273)

The novices at Lincoln used several phrases like the ones in these two examples to describe how their mentors/coaches protected them from stress and perceived conflict with school leaders, students, and colleagues. It was unfortunate that mentors/coaches and novices at Lincoln believed that such protection was necessary. Also, I noticed some evidence of triangulation when mentors/coachs took their novices' sides against administrators. For example, Mrs. Stanley, Mrs. Lawson's mentor/coach had some rather strong metaphors to describe her perceptions of the relationship between the administration and her mentee.

> **Tip #2:** If collegial partners perceive that protection is often necessary at their school, they might participate in conversations that may include all parties and that revolve around these kinds of questions:
>
> - What behavior or behaviors are creating problems between novices/struggling teachers and others?
> - Why are such behaviors a problem?
> - What can each person involved in the problem do to address it?
> - How might a neutral party help to address the problem?

- ♦ What might happen if the problem behavior or behaviors persist?
- ♦ What resources might be useful to resolve the problems?

If all parties have a commitment to a "win-win" solution (i.e., everyone involved is satisfied with the problem resolution), then they are more likely to determine solutions that work for everyone. Partners might also become familiar with the concept of triangulation so that they might notice if they have not stayed neutral or have taken sides in a conflict. When an entire school makes a commitment to learning and practicing good conflict resolution skills, the need for protection should be minimal.

Authentic Professional Dialogue

Acknowledgement

When collegial partnerships use authentic professional dialogue, which can include complex conversations, they seem to be able to resolve many of the conflicts they might experience in their schools. Acknowledging the strengths and contributions of colleagues seems useful in terms of building trust and promoting an appreciative (e.g. Cooperrider et al., 2007) versus a deficit response (Gold, 1996). The major caution partnerships may consider is that acknowledgement is fundamentally different from praise, mainly because praise can be perceived as evaluative and evidence of a power differential whereas acknowledgement stands a better chance of seeming like an exchange of information between equals. For example, a message that begins, "I am proud of you …" or "You did a good job when you …" can place the person making the statement on a higher power level than the person they are proud of or complimenting. Acknowledgement provides a way to avoid this possible power-over assumption because the message identifies specific instances of accomplishment. Starting sentences with, "I appreciate the way you …" or "Can I steal this (specific idea) from you because …? focuses on the speaker rather than the person being spoken about and seems less like evaluation and more like acknowledgement.

Avoiding a Deficit Perspective

Acknowledgment is a great antidote to what Gold (1996) refers to as a deficit perspective. Gold suggested that a deficit perspective assumes that novices and struggling teachers are ill-prepared through teacher education programs and thus need mentoring and coaching to help them survive in their schools. On the other hand, she suggested that if educators see mentoring and coaching as a step in a continuum of professional development services, then mentoring and coaching support might address differing levels of novice teachers' needs for professional growth and development that might take them beyond merely surviving their first year. These lessons learned in the first years are critical to novices and struggling teachers, being able to develop the characteristics that sustain professionalism and commitment to teaching.

Acknowledgement at Lincoln High School

I found many examples of mentors/coaches and novices acknowledging the skills and knowledge of each other. Here are some examples:

- Mr. Manzetti (mentor) said that Mrs. Baker (novice) used more creative approaches to teaching their curriculum than he did, and Mrs. Baker acknowledged Mr. Manzetti's trustworthy nature.
- Mrs. Herman (mentor/coach) said that Mr. Cook (novice) took ideas from her and put his own twist on them so that she hardly recognized them as hers, and Mr. Cook said that Mrs. Herman worked harder than anyone else at their school.
- Ms. Captain (novice) acknowledged Mrs. Rankin's (mentor) constant positive attitude, and Mrs. Rankin acknowledged Ms. Captain's depth of knowledge regarding her content and her ability to convey that content knowledge via technology.
- Mrs. Truitt (mentor) was impressed with the way Mr. Hansen's (novice) demeanor was effective with advanced students, and Mr. Hansen acknowledged Mrs. Truitt by nominating her for "Mentor of the Year."

All of these examples show that acknowledgment of achievement went both ways between mentors/coaches and novices and did not sound like praise.

> **Tip #3:** School leaders can model acknowledgment in their day-to-day conversations with faculty and staff. They might also create events that model acknowledgment. For example, they might use typical acknowledgment processes like "Teacher of the Week/Month/Year." They might also use processes that are more personal. For example, just as principals often recommend that teachers make "positive calls" to their students'

parents, school leaders might also make a point of trying to send positive messages or make positive oral comments to teachers and staff at least once per semester and more often if the teacher is struggling. Collegial partners might also get into a habit of acknowledging each other for specific positive behaviors.

Advocacy

Another useful technique within authentic professional dialogue is advocacy, which is the process by which collegial partners promote certain practices or behaviors. Advocacy differs from advice-giving, because those who use it present it in terms of self-disclosure or answers to questions about challenges that one peer offers another. Advising can be risky. It is much safer to share personal experiences or knowledge. Avoiding advice-giving can be very difficult and sometimes it seems that those with whom we work actually want our advice. Even when it is solicited, advice can be tricky because if someone gives specific advice rather than helping the other person come to his or her own conclusions about what to do, the advisee might blame the advisor if the advice is not helpful. Also, using a process of inquiry, which I will discuss next, helps the person make his or her own decisions about solutions. In this book, I provide tips, which some might view as advice-giving. I hope I made it clear in my introduction that I base my tips on my experiences, the literature, and my research. I do not claim that they are "best practices" that will resolve everyone's problems. In other words, I am not intending to advise; I am disclosing ideas that *could* be helpful, depending on the situation.

Advocacy at Lincoln High School

Mentors/coaches at Lincoln used advocacy often. They may also have given advice, but I did not notice it in the interviews I conducted. Some of the practices they advocated were similar, such as encouraging novices/struggling teachers to handle their discipline issues in-house; others were highly specific. For example, Mrs. Truitt shared with Mr. Hansen how well it worked to get face-to-face with students when she was talking to them, and she explored with Mr. Hansen how he might consider bending down to make sure his height (over six feet) did not prevent him from getting face-to-face with his students. In general, mentors/coaches at Lincoln helped novices understand the school culture by advocating certain practices that aligned or did not align with that culture. In this way, they helped novices make decisions about their practices that fit into that culture rather than going against it.

> **Tip #4:** Replacing unsolicited advice-giving and notions of best practices with advocacy helps make collegial partnerships peer-to-peer rather than superior-to-subordinate. For example, saying something like, "When I had to deal with ... in our curriculum, I found that ... worked well in my class" is more helpful than saying something like, "When you teach ... you should use ...." Avoiding advice-giving is great in theory; however, it is not easy to do and takes a great deal of commitment and practice.

Inquiry and Invitation

Being genuinely curious about the thoughts and feelings of another person undergirds the practices of inquiry within professional dialogue. Some of the most successful conversations emerge from well-crafted questions that convey a deep sense of curiosity and that help others explore their concerns. When collegial partners have a sincere interest in and the capacity to use inquiry in professional dialogue, they appear to be able to make progress in developing sound practices and handling school conflicts. Inquiry goes beyond questioning to also include wondering and imagining with others.

Invitation is the aspect of authentic professional dialogue that helps participants help each other through mutuality rather than hierarchy. For example, the process of inviting a response from another person makes collaborative conversation possible and it helps prevent unsolicited advice-giving. In addition, those who feel invited to participate in something are more likely to develop a sense of belonging and more likely to feel that the person inviting them is truly interested in hearing what they have to say. Partners who use invitation within professional dialogue have the potential for sharing ideas that can improve their practices and help them handle school conflicts.

Inquiry and invitation also can help to address one of the major barriers to conflict resolution: denial. If individuals or entire school systems deny that certain conflicts exist, those conflicts do not go away, and they can erode relationships within the school. If school leaders and partnerships use the processes of inquiry and invitation, they show that it is safe to bring out conflicts that those in less healthy systems might deny.

Inquiry and Invitation at Lincoln High School

An excellent example of inquiry occurred when Mrs. Herman (mentor/coach) used it to help Mrs. Baker (novice) explore why her students were having problems passing her class. The questions Mrs. Herman asked demonstrated that she understood what was happening, and they guided Mrs. Baker toward awareness of her role in the students' failure. Novices/struggling teachers also used inquiry when they asked their mentors/coaches and other colleagues how they handled certain situations or taught certain content.

The mentors/coaches and novices at Lincoln used invitation often within their professional dialogue, such as when a mentor/coach invited a novice to share lesson plans. They created a safe space for venting frustrations and made themselves available for novices.

Unfortunately, I did encounter some instances of denial at Lincoln. For example, the school and the district seemed to deny some of the fundamental concerns that may have contributed to the constant turnover of teachers.

> **Tip #5:** The precedent for incorporating inquiry and invitation into professional dialogue is set through the modeling of those who understand how to use them. For example, during faculty meetings, school leaders skilled in the use of inquiry and invitation might use words such as "we invite your responses" and they might also model a sincere curiosity regarding the thoughts and feelings of the faculty and staff. At the beginning of the year, many school leaders tell faculty and staff that they have an "open door policy," and they invite faculty and staff to share their concerns whenever they feel it is important. Of course, school leaders cannot possibly attend to every concern that faculty and staff might have; therefore, that offer of an open door could assume that faculty and staff will reserve it for the most important conversations. Unfortunately, sometimes novices and struggling teachers, who have many occasions to need help, do not understand that it is not feasible for school leaders to hear from them often. It might be more helpful for them to hear from administrators that before coming to their door, they might want to first check with their mentors/coaches or a trusted colleague. Mentors and coaches might reassure novices and struggling teachers that they will be able to help as an alternative to going to the principal, and novices and struggling teachers might consider only going to the office if their mentors or coaches suggest it. Finally, collegial partners might pay attention to any evidence that denial is at work within their relationships, their school, or their district. If they realize denial is a factor, they might use invitation and inquiry within professional dialogue to better understand the realities and then to address them directly.

Collaborative Culture

According to Himmelman (1994, 2001), collaboration is the most effective tool for sharing resources, resolving problems, and creating sustainable change. The concept of collaboration is a term that most people use, but not everyone agrees on what it means. From my perspective, the people who decide to work together in order to help one another are the ones who mutually define collaboration and collaborative cultures. Himmelman offered some useful ideas. For example, he explained a progression of increasingly risky steps that move a group toward collaboration. Although I would propose that the progression may not always be linear and hierarchical so that the behaviors might occur in complex ways rather than linear ones, I agree that collaboration includes some of the types of behaviors Himmelman described. Himmelman said that these steps begin with networking and then move to coordination, next to cooperation, and finally to collaboration. In networking, a group makes a commitment to share information for mutual benefit. In coordination, the group not only exchanges information but also adjusts its activities to address a common purpose. In cooperation, groups not only share information and change their activities for a common purpose but also commit to sharing resources. Finally, in collaboration, they share information, adjust activities for a common purpose, and share resources, but they do all of these things to help each other build capacity. Ideally, the collegial partnerships should reflect all of these behaviors because a major aspect of these relationships is enhancing the capacity of one another. It seems reasonable that collaborative relationships could function most smoothly in a school culture that is also collaborative. This notion of collaborative culture, therefore, aligns with or could be another way of expressing the notion of a culture of helping.

Collaborative Culture at Lincoln

I have already explained in detail how learning communities functioned at Lincoln. Although the school leadership required each department to hold learning community meetings for the purpose of collaborating, collaboration was not consistent at the school. My research participants said that some departments used learning community time to share important tasks that made their jobs easier and more aligned, whereas others used their learning community time as a gripe session. They seemed to believe that the fact that some collaborative communities were better than others had less to do with the manner in which the leadership had set up the process and more to do with the individual personalities of those who were in charge of providing the leadership for the community. Due to the inconsistencies in the implementation of learning communities at Lincoln High School, I wondered if school leaders had provided adequate training, monitoring, and support regarding how to use them for collaboration.

Tip #6: If school leaders are committed to using learning communies to establish a collaborative culture, they may strongly consider providing comprehensive training to get them started, monitoring to make sure they are functioning properly, and support to make sure all involved have what they need. As far as training is concerned, school leaders might use a variety of resources about learning communities, including book study groups or outside consultants. In terms of monitoring, if the entire school or several departments or grade levels are not functioning as a collaborative culture, school leaders might consider having some complex conversations with any groups that *are* collaborating and those that are not. Some of the important questions school leaders may choose to ask members of the various learning communities include the following:

- What collaborative contributions are you making to your learning community?
- How are you enhancing the capacity of your fellow colleagues?

As far as support for those who are not collaborating in their learning community, school leaders might ask individuals, privately or in groups, these questions:

- What do you need from school leaders to help your department (or grade level) establish a collaborative culture?
- What do you need from school leaders, and what are you willing to contribute to help make this school a collaborative culture?

Shared Understandings

Shared understandings are an aspect of ecologically based capacity building in which members of a group have common beliefs that allow them to better work together. I thoroughly covered this topic in Chapter 6 when I explained some of the redundancies (similarities) between collegial partners, and the only thing to add here is that having these shared understandings helps build sustained capacity within relationships. They also provide a common ground for the entire school culture.

Shared Understandings at Lincoln

Although I already covered the major shared understandings among the members of my study, I was interested to note some ideas about the kinds of teachers who could make it at their school. Although these specific perspectives were not as common among the faculty, they were, nevertheless, important in terms of views of teaching at Lincoln. For example,

> Mrs. Stewart had never thought of quitting teaching because she had always "wanted for [her] whole life" to become a teacher, but she *had* thought of "giving up." For example, she had thought of just "biding [her] time" or possibly leaving for a while to go to graduate school. She said she sees her colleagues doing their "prescripted jobs" that included doing "just enough until they have to go home again." It had "crossed [her] mind" that she did not have to put up with the disrespect, she did not have to take students into the hallway and "work out a relationship," and she did not have to "put up with their crap" because she could do like her colleagues and "ship them to ISS (In School Suspension) and not have them in her room." But she realized if she decided to bide her time, no one would know but her kids, and "that [was] what [kept her] going" that they would "know if [she] gave up. …
> "Mrs. Stewart decided that to be successful with the students in her school, a teacher had to be 'consistently pursuing them' and that teachers who did not do well were 'not in pursuit of their students.'" (Waterman, 2012, p. 295)

Another perspective from Mrs. Herman was powerful:

> The students at Lincoln needed "a lot of love" and care, but many of their teachers could not reach them or in some cases were "intimidated" by them because these students were often suspicious and cautious and "would fight a teacher" they thought was "not fair." These kinds of teachers were not successful at Lincoln. (Waterman, 2012, p. 280)

Tip #7: Teachers enter schools with ideas about teaching practices that come from deeply-held values and from their pre-service experiences; however, school leaders and peers can have a strong influence on the emergence and development of new beliefs. I have already discussed how school leaders, faculty, and staff might work together to clarify the dominant values and beliefs that inform the practices at the school. This is an important step if school leaders and peers want to convey those values and beliefs to the new hires in the school. If school leaders and peers do a good job of practicing their values and beliefs, they should be able to influence new faculty and staff to share those beliefs. Also, if school leaders expect regular observations among peers, active participation in learning communities, study groups that investigate topics of mutual interest, and a variety of opportunities for professional development, then it seems more likely that faculty and staff will develop a strong set of shared understandings.

Synchronicity

According to Jung (1960), who coined the term, synchronicity is an event that seems to occur without cause, but seems important. Jaworski (1996) took the idea further when he based his notion of synchronicity on the work of David Bohm (1980). According to Jaworski and Bohm, there is an implicate order that exists beyond our awareness. Some refer to this idea of an implicate order as the forces of the universe with which we are all connected. This connection is similar to connections within the explicate order, which includes close connections with entities we can observe, such as the connection between mentors/coaches and novices/struggling teachers. Our connection with the implicate order (or the universe) helps explain synchronistic events that seem to happen just at the right time and that mean a great deal to us.

"Swimming in the Land of the Lost"

I was unable to gather many examples of synchronicity from most of my research participants, but Mrs. Stewart (novice) provided a wonderful example.

> Mrs. Herman collaborated with the person from the central office who was in charge of over-seeing [a special curriculum] and together they told Mrs. Stewart that she was a "passionate teacher with charisma." This kind of positive acknowledgement of her abilities seemed to always come when Mrs. Stewart felt she was "swimming in the land of the lost," and it was ironic that this encouragement came when she felt she was "sinking." (Waterman, 2012, p. 322)

Mrs. Stewart had a strong connection with Mrs. Herman, and it showed up in this example of synchronicity. Other evidence of their strong connection showed when they co-constructed a metaphor to describe their "hormonal" students. I could tell that they were on the same wavelength by the way they completed each other's sentences and laughed when they shared similar ideas.

> **Tip #8:** Synchronicity is similar to the *teachable moments* and *space for emergence* that I explained in Chapter 2. According to Jaworski (1996), leaders might elicit synchronicity if they stay open to the possibility of its benefits, and collegial partners can develop attitudes and behaviors that allow learning to emerge through planned activities suggested in this book. Policies and procedures established within the school can show the value of meeting in dyads or in groups for the purpose of participating in activities that elicit synchronicity. Also, in order to help teachers learn to recognize and appreciate synchronicity, school leaders might explain it by providing examples from their own lives. They could then make time at every faculty meeting for teachers to share synchronistic moments that made a difference in their teaching practices; how they related to a colleague, student, or parent; or a variety of other important aspects of professional teaching. Some faculties might be more open than others and some cultural groups might be more amenable to attributing instances of synchronicity to powers beyond what we might rationally prove. Keeping an open mind is a good practice, in general, and if school leaders believe that acknowledging instances of synchronicity might contribute to the possibilities that colleagues will gain a sense of unity, then why not entertain the possibility that forces in the universe might play a role? Finally, school leaders might consider investigating a relatively new technique that can help faculty and staff become more open to a kind of learning that extends beyond traditional methods. This technique, called the Theory of the U, comes from Senge, Scharmer, Jaworski, and Flowers (2004).

The Theory of the U

According to Senge et al. (2004), the U movement, which is an extension of all learning processes, has three basic aspects and seven capacities. (See Figure 7.2). The top left of the U is "sensing," during which we "download our mental models" in order to determine what we are able to see with our perspective; that is, we observe. The bottom of the U is "presencing," during which we reflect and let knowledge emerge. The top right of the U is "realizing," during which we act without hesitating if we are going with the flow (p. 88).

Also included on the three phases of the U are seven capacities involved in learning. First, during the sensing phase of the U, we use the capacities of "suspending" and "redirecting." When we suspend our thinking, we observe our own perspective and we "redirect" by seeing from the perspective of the whole complex system. Next, during the presencing phase, we "let go" so that we can allow new learning and experiences come to us. In the final phase, "realizing," we experiment with prototypes of our innovative ideas to see which ones are viable. We also crystallize those thoughts that emerged and those that we envision as possibilities. Last of all we institutionalize our new ideas, making them reality. In sum, the U theory suggests that by going through its various levels in the correct order, those involved in learning and changing will develop "a new capacity for observing that no longer fragments the observer from what's observed; a new capacity for stillness that no longer fragments who we really are from what's emerging; and a new capacity for creating alternative realities that no longer fragments the wisdom of the head, heart, and hand" (p. 212).

The Theory of the U identifies specific processes that the other models seem to have left out. For example, although Mitchell and Sackney (2001, 2009) provided useful applications of complex thinking to ecologically based

Figure 7.2 The Theory of the U Graphic

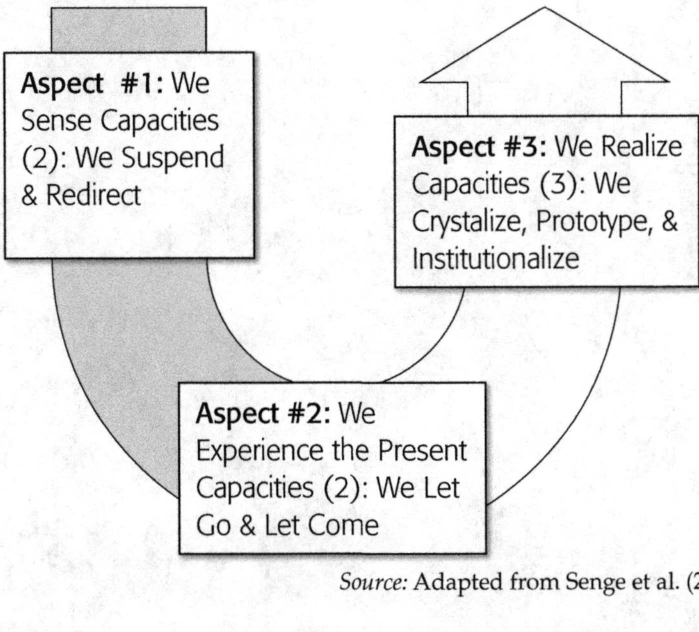

Source: Adapted from Senge et al. (2004, p. 219)

sustainable capacity building in terms of developing learning communities, they stopped short of providing a specific and clear model. The Theory of the U provides such a model. Specifically, Senge et al. (2004) showed how in a stepwise fashion mentors/coaches and novices/struggling teachers might go through the processes involved in the U to create "alternate realities" that are open to synchronicity (p. 212).

Saving Time and Money

A school culture that understands and implements ecologically based sustainable capacity building can expect to save more time and money each year. This is because they are learning how to make the best use of all of their resources—human and material. Schools that are building capacity have fewer needs to replace human resources because fewer faculty and staff leave their schools. They also have fewer needs to take time out for and to pay for outside resources because they are learning to be self-sufficient. As a self-sufficient culture, they can use their time and money for enhancing their capacities rather than for catching up or remediating a broken system.

Activities

Collaboration PowerPoint Outline

Here is an outline for a twenty-slide PowerPoint presentation I developed about collaboration. To use this outline, add some interesting pictures, and you will have a useful presentation to make to faculty or smaller groups.

What Is Collaboration?	
Slide 1: What is collaboration?	**Slide 2:** It is not ... just sitting in a room with a variety of people
Slide 3: It is ... creating whole new ways of interacting with each other	**Slide 4:** Collaboration can ... maximize resources
Slide 5: Find solutions ... to intractable problems	**Slide 6:** Create revolutionary changes ... in our community and the world
Slide 7: Four Kinds of Group Exchanges ♦ networking ♦ coordination ♦ cooperation ♦ collaboration	**Slide 8:** Continuum of Functions of Exchanges Low Risk → High Risk Networking, Coordinating, Cooperating, Collaborating
Slide 9: Increasing ... risks, commitment, and contribution of resources increase the capacity for change	**Slide 10:** Collaboration is ... the most powerful tool for community change
Slide 11: Building Blocks for Collaboration: ♦ networking ♦ exchanging information for mutual benefit	**Slide 12:** Coordinating exchanging information and altering activities for mutual benefit and a common purpose
Slide 13: Cooperating exchanging information, altering activities, and sharing resources for mutual benefit and to achieve a common purpose	**Slide 14:** Collaborating exchanging information, altering activities, sharing resources for mutual benefit to achieve a common purpose and to enhance the capacity of another

(continued)

What Is Collaboration?	
Slide 15: Managing the 4 Rs RISKS *Key Question:* If we take this risk together, will we approach the consequences in the same way?	**Slide 16:** RESOURCES *Key Questions:* Who gets the resources? Who determines how they will be used?
Slide 17: REWARDS *Key Question:* How will we share the sense of accomplishment?	**Slide 18:** RESPONSIBITIES *Key Question:* How can we ensure that everyone equally shares responsibility?
Slide 19: How Do We Want To Collaborate in Our School?	**Slide 20:** References Tom Wolff & Associates. (2005). *Collaborative solutions: True collaboration as the most productive form of change.* Retrieved May 24, 2012, from http://tomwolff.com/collaborative-solutions-newsletter-summer-05.htm. *Primary Sources:* Himmelman, A. (2001). On coalitions and the transformation of power relations: Collaborative betterment and collaborative empowerment. *American Journal of Community Psychology, 29*(2), pp. 277–285. Himmellman, A. (1994). Communities working collaboratively for change. In *Resolving conflict: Strategies for local government.* M. Herrman (ed.) pp. 27–47. Washington, DC: International City/County Management Association.

Creating a Container #2

What follows is another way of developing a "container"—a safe place in which people who work in groups might have authentic dialogue (Isaacs, 1999, p. 242). Isaacs's processes differ somewhat from those presented by Mitchell and Sackney (2009) and Pratt (2008); nevertheless, I present them here as useful techniques to consider. Isaacs determined that members of a group need to thoroughly understand and practice four core skills if they want to build their capacity to create containers for deep and honest dialogue. Those four skills are listening, respecting, suspending, and voicing. I will present an overview of these skills; however, to more deeply understand them, I suggest your group consider studying Isaacs's book before or during the process of attempting to implement these practices.

Those who wish to develop a "container" may present the following contract-like information to potential group members.

The _______________ (identifying name) Container

As a member of this container, I promise to:

- ♦ participate in study group sessions around developing a safe container
- ♦ attend regularly scheduled meetings unless I am physically unable to do so
- ♦ take personal responsibility for working with others to maintain the safety and usefulness of the container
- ♦ learn to utilize the four core processes that we will enact in our container

1. Listening – I will listen carefully and responsibly to what fellow container members say. I will be sensitive to the dilemmas they face, and I will avoid objectifying any member of the group.
2. Respecting – I will, above all, be respectful in my attitudes toward each container member. I will learn to "hold the tension" (Isaacs, 1999, p. 130) that might exist when our perspectives clash so that I might learn more about the others' perspectives. I will avoid "conversational violence" (p. 132), which is the opposite of respect.
3. Suspending – I will neither reject what I think nor reject what fellow container members think. I will not advocate my perspective unilaterally, but I will show what I am thinking so that others might come to understand it and see what I mean. I will reflect on what is going on while it is happening. I will not hold on to a need to be certain.
4. Voicing – I will responsibly and authentically express myself to fellow container members. I will "overcome self-censorship" (p.169), and I will use my own stories to co-create with fellow group members. I will not speak too much or too little.

Signed_______________________________ Date___________________

Invitations

Creating an inviting school culture is a useful goal. Collegial partners, school leaders, and peers might send "cards" inviting novices/struggling teachers and others to attend important school functions. This kind of activity will not work if the invitation is not really an invitation, but a command. We hope that those involved in our meetings will want to attend them, but if they do not, we may need to rethink the purpose of the meeting.

Surveys

SurveyMonkey (2012) has job satisfaction surveys that those who want to understand how teachers are feeling about their jobs might access. Using surveys is an easy method for finding out ways to improve an organization. SurveyMonkey offers three tips for using a survey to assess job satisfaction:

- ♦ Employees need to trust that their responses are confidential.
- ♦ Make sure that everyone is willing to complete the survey, or the results will be invalid.
- ♦ Ask questions about how well employees understand employers' expectations, how those expectations might challenge them, and what they might recommend.

SurveyMonkey has pre-made surveys that can examine the following topics: Employee Job Satisfaction, Career Training and Development, Self-Assessment, Employee Satisfaction with the Company, and Employee Satisfaction with Personnel Policies.

CHAPTER 8

Eleven Final Tips for Decision Makers and Practitioners

I hope you have found some useful ideas in this book to adjust and adapt to match the needs of your organization and its members. One of the main ideas that emerged from my study was that all educational stakeholders would be wise to consider complexity when they plan and implement mentoring/coaching initiatives. As I mentioned in the introduction, I believe that many of the topics I have explored in this book assume that *planning for complexity* may help to bring about the emergence of a culture of helping. At this point, I review the concept of planning for complexity.

Planning for Complexity

Planning for complexity aligns with ideas from soft science organizational theorists, such as Stacey (1992), and from hard science theorists such as Prigogine and Stengers (1984). These complexity theorists addressed the problems that organizations (like schools) face when they attempt to know the unknowable. They propose that traditionally we tend to think in terms of "either or," but if we think in terms of complexity we think in terms of "both and" (Stacey, 1992, p. 19). This means that both formal and centralized structures and behaviors coexist with emergent and unstable structures and behaviors. The essence of this thinking is that we need both structure (plans) and flexibility (attention to emergence) in order to develop mentoring/coaching initiatives that stand a good chance of being useful to those who implement them.

In the spirit of planning for complexity, I include here some final tips for decision makers and practitioners. The suggestions I make revolve around

Figure 8.1 Decision-Maker Topics

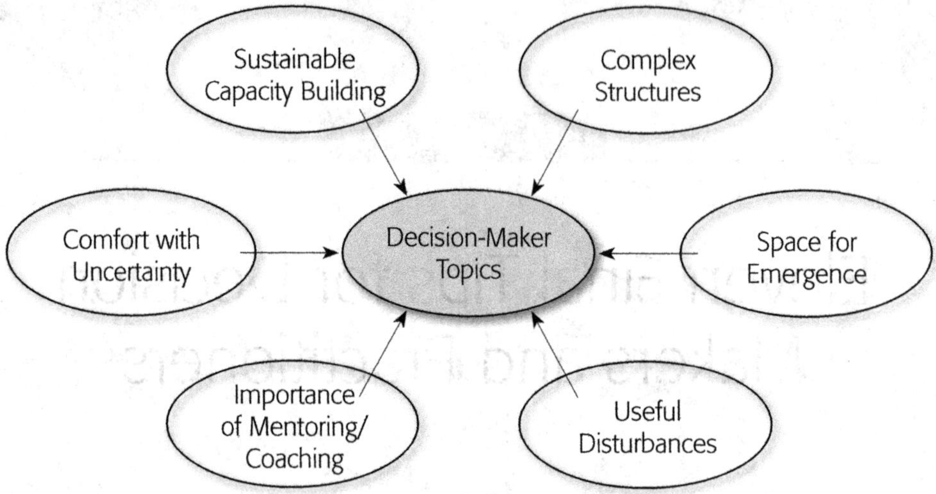

several topics for decision makers, such as comfort with uncertainty, sustainable capacity building, complex structures, space for emergence, useful disturbances, and the importance of mentoring/coaching, (see Figure 8.1). The topics I address for practitioners are mentor identity, flexibility, redundancy and diversity, decentralized decision, and sustainable capacity building. (See Figure 8.3, page 158.)

Comfort with Uncertainty

The first step toward developing comfort with uncertainty is acknowledging that even though human systems are complex, we can still function if we are uncertain how our plans will turn out. Remaining open to surprises and the emergence of responses that hopefully address problems, but just as easily might create them, can help decision makers avoid considerable frustration and negativity. For example, when decision makers attempt to make a difference in a complex system, they can see any response, even if it seems negative, as an opportunity for growth rather than failure. Changing the way they think about complex human systems and changing their attitudes about them may need to come before changing how they talk about addressing those systems. Then once they understand the limitations of certainty, decision makers use language like "We are making plans to ..." instead of "We are going to. ..." By using the first statement, decision makers convey the idea that they will leave open the possibility that a person, people, or the system might drastically change their plans. And that is all right! Changing their thoughts, attitudes, and words can help decision makers feel more comfortable with uncertainty.

Tip #1: Educators who understand the process of planning for complexity need to evaluate their comfort with uncertainty. In order to do this, they might reflect on their thinking, their attitudes, and the words they use to express that comfort. If they are planning the policies and procedures for a mentoring and coaching program, they may even ask an outside evaluator to help them make sure they are heading in the right direction. Some questions to consider are as follows:

- Have we invited those most affected by our mentoring/coaching policies to participate in decision making?
- Have we avoided making unilateral decisions that affect those involved in implementing our programs?
- Are we open to the possibility that other stakeholders may have ideas that conflict with ours? If so what will we do about that?
- Are we comfortable with results that could be better than expected or worse?

These kinds of questions can inspire the development of plans for mentoring and coaching policies and procedures that extend beyond traditional ideas.

Sustainable Capacity Building

The three processes: (1) collegial dynamics that members practice within (2) collaborative cultures and that they base on (3) shared understandings allow organizations to develop sustainable learning communities (Mitchell & Sackney, 2009). Learning communities developed using these three processes stand a good chance of promoting the emergence of a culture of helping that supports and enhances the relationships within collegial partnerships. Some specific collegial dynamics, for example, include acknowledgement, advocacy, inquiry, and invitation, and they are specifically useful for mentoring and coaching programs. It is also important that decision makers keep themselves open to synchronicity, which can deepen relationships and facilitate a culture of helping.

Tip #2: If decision makers are interested in sustaining school improvement, they may consider making plans to promote ecologically based capacity-building processes in their schools. One of the best ways for decision makers to promote collegial dynamics is by modeling them through their own personal and group behaviors and by setting up structures that support them. For example, decision makers might engage in authentic professional dialogue that includes acknowledgment, advocacy, inquiry, and invitation—with other decision makers and with members of faculties and staffs. They might also use faculty meetings, other school meetings, or virtual communications to inform faculties and staffs about the usefulness of collegial dynamics. They might also find ways to constantly evaluate their own use of these dynamics and to help others monitor their use of them.

In terms of establishing a collaborative culture that supports helping relationships within the school, decision makers might establish the use of professional dialogue and complex conversation to continually determine how faculties and staffs are working together to establish this culture. Decision makers might find ways to establish a collaborative school culture if they recognize their power to promote that culture or interfere with it. For example, they might allocate more resources to teams that demonstrate collaboration, and they might recognize personal and group behaviors that exemplify it. Foremost, they should not assume that just because they say they want a collaborative culture that everyone in the school will understand what that means. Decision makers who want to promote a collaborative culture first need to have a strong vision of what it can look like at their schools, but then they must also help others understand that vision, experience it first hand, and practice it over and over again until it truly becomes "the culture" of the school, not just a series of fragmented initiatives.

To address shared understandings, decision makers may devise strategies for discovering the shared understandings that affect behaviors in the school. They should not assume that just because a group makes a list of shared values and beliefs, those are the only values and beliefs at work in the school. Decision makers may learn to become sensitive to behaviors that may indicate a shared understanding that is having a negative effect on the school culture. When they find out what that understanding is, they might then participate in authentic professional dialogue to learn where it came from and how they might take steps to address it so that it does not continue to feed negative behaviors.

To promote synchronicity in their schools, decision makers might learn processes detailed in "The Theory of the U." I suggest Senge et al. (2004) and Jaworski (1996) to get a more thorough understanding of how organizations might access forces beyond what one might explain rationally. Reading those books and looking for examples of synchronicity can help decision makers think outside the box when it comes to developing sustainable new capacities within their schools.

Specifically related to mentoring and coaching programs, decision makers might continually monitor how the school is implementing those programs and if the program design matches the needs of the school. If the program design does not match the context in which collegial partnerships implement it, decision makers might meet with stakeholders, especially partners, to determine how to adjust it. For example, at Lincoln, teacher turnover was so constant that the school often did not have enough "trained" mentors to help all the new teachers; therefore, Lincoln used untrained mentors. The fact that an untrained mentor did such a good job that her mentee nominated her for "Mentor of the Year" leads to these questions: Was mentor training necessary? What might qualify someone to be a useful mentor or coach? Decision makers in this case might have conversations with the relevant stakeholders to evaluate their training programs and their policies about using trained mentors in certain schools where the need is so high.

Complex Structures

In Chapters 1–6, I described, exemplified, and suggested tips about how mentoring/coaching programs function as complex systems. For example, I explained in detail the manner in which the context had a relationship with collegial partnerships. These relationships are self-organized, short-ranged, closed, decentralized, and structure-determined. The overarching conclusion I reached based on the nature of mentoring and coaching as complex systems was that although all complex systems have these common structures and functions, each complex system enacts them in unique ways. In other words, the nature of partnerships is both determined and undetermined at the same time.

> **Tip #3:** Decision makers who are familiar with the structures and functions of complex systems will use that knowledge to help them plan mentoring and coaching initiatives that acknowledge the features of complex systems. With this knowledge, they might develop general guidelines for mentoring and coaching programs that reflect complex structures and functions, keeping in mind that those structures and functions are constantly moving and changing. In other words, their programs will acknowledge that collegial partnerships will perform structures and functions in a unique manner. One of the best examples of this process occurs if decision makers require schools to assign temporary mentors and coaches but then give novices and struggling teachers a chance to choose their own

after a transition period has passed. In this way, they institute structures within which people can determine their own ways of functioning. Decision makers might also resist the assumption that they know best what partnerships need to discuss; however, they might ask for clear evidence that partners are learning new practices and improving their skills.

Space for Emergence

One of the most powerful structures decision makers might incorporate in the school culture is the notion of space for emergence that provides room for members of a complex system to build capacity and learn (Davis & Sumara, 2006). Organizational theorist Wheatley (2006) suggested that organizations that resist the need to exert tight controls over their employees stand a better chance of developing members who are loyal, creative, and productive. Other organizational theorists have proposed loosening controls over employees through the structuring of spaces for the emergence of solutions to problems that have an effect on the organizations and on individuals within the organizations (DuFour & Eaker, 1998; Waterman, 1987; Weick, 1976). For example, Waterman (1987, no relation) suggested a "solution space" in which employers provide a place and a cultural norm that demonstrates the belief in the power of employees to find creative solutions to company problems (p. 90). Decision makers who develop an appreciative rather than a deficit perspective are often pleased with the results. This does not mean that this space is limitless. For example, decision makers may not feel comfortable leaving every group to its own devices; therefore, the implementation of a space for emergence is still a dance between tight controls and loose ones. Depending on the group and the tasks, the space may need monitoring and inputting of resources to help it along.

Tip #4: Decision makers may consider establishing the following structures:

- ♦ a temporary, formally assigned mentor or coach, with the understanding that the novice or struggling teacher will find his/her own permanent collegial partner within a designated time period
- ♦ a time in the school day when partnerships might meet
- ♦ a school norm that prioritizes a safe space where partnerships can have authentic professional dialogue
- ♦ evidence that partners are making progress in their work

Within these structures, decision makers may afford partnerships the capacity to determine for themselves how they will function within those structures. For example, partners may decide to continue their temporary assignment or change it, they may do what they think is best in the time and place they have set aside to meet, and they may decide what evidence they will present to show that they are making progress. Decision makers, in collaboration with partners, may determine that some training around techniques such as acknowledgment, advocacy, inquiry, and invitation could be useful to them.

Useful Disturbances

Decision makers must understand on a deep level that they cannot cause or motivate employees to do what they want them to do. Instead, they might create triggers or disturbances that could inspire employees to respond in ways those employees see fit and in which they are capable (Capra, 2002). Acknowledging that their plans do not cause a specific reaction from complex human systems, decision makers can avoid becoming defensive if those charged with implementing their decisions do not implement them with fidelity or do not implement them at all. Defensiveness or denial of the problems that can arise when decisions made globally do not work well locally can shut down authentic professional dialogue. Respect for the integrity of those implementing decisions suggests that decision makers might include in their decisions the perspectives of a wide range of those who will implement their decisions. It also suggests that decision makers develop a comprehensive understanding of the group for whom they are making decisions so that they plan for the capacities and interests of those they want to implement their plans.

Tip #5: If decision makers avoid defensiveness and denial, they will be better able to make sure lines of communication stay open to make appropriate changes or adjustments in their plans. By remaining open, they will be better able to determine which of their ideas are welcome by their employees and which are unwelcome. For example, decision makers may plan a training day on complexity thinking that their employees may not welcome, but these employees *may* welcome instead a free day to plan and improve their teamwork. That said, it can also be important that decision makers who understand the need for a balance between comfort and challenge may need to strongly promote some unwelcome disturbances that could be necessary to shake up some unhealthy or misguided practices standing in the way of school improvement. By keeping the lines of communication open, these decision makers stand a better chance of pushing through some of their less popular, but useful ideas.

The Importance of Mentors and Coaches

Although recent research has challenged the usefulness of mentoring and coaching to improve teachers' practices and reduce teacher turnover (Guarino, Santibanez, & Daley, 2006; Waterman & He, 2011), decision makers should realize that some research methods are unable to capture the effects of complex systems such as collegial partnerships. For example, in my study, it was apparent that mentors and coaches were highly important to the novices I interviewed. The story of Mr. Cook's almost quitting but first consulting his mentor/coach, Mrs. Herman, shows that even if mentors and coaches may not make a difference in all of the decisions that novice and struggling teachers make, they can sometimes make a significant difference. One of the major findings of my study, which is also the finding of other studies of mentoring (e.g., Guarino et al., 2006) was that the connection between mentoring and novices' decisions to stay in or leave a school are inconclusive. I contend further that the complexity of the partnership makes it impossible to ascribe reasons based on that relationship that teachers might stay or leave the profession.

I used the following conceptual framework to try to better understand what conflicts might trigger the movement of a novice toward or away from a school or the profession (Waterman, 2012, p. 46). (See Figure 8.2.) What I discovered was that the complexity of the situation made ascribing reasons difficult if not impossible. This discovery questions the notion that certain reasons might drive teachers from the profession or keep them in it. I simply could not tell why the majority of the novices I studied left Lincoln.

Tip #6: Although I concluded that it is difficult, if not impossible, to tell why teachers leave certain schools and what roles their mentors and coaches might play in those decisions, I do contend that mentoring and coaching are useful for novices and struggling teachers. Instead of focusing on whether or how collegial partners might make a difference in teachers' decisions to leave a school, decision makers should focus on using them as colleagues they trust to help them convey the school's values and its culture to novices and struggling teachers. By bonding with partners, decision makers might better plan supportive programs for novices and struggling teachers so that they will eventually become successful at the school. Or if these teachers seem misplaced at the school, their partners can help decision makers counsel them to find an environment that may better fit their needs.

Figure 8.2 My Conceptual Framework

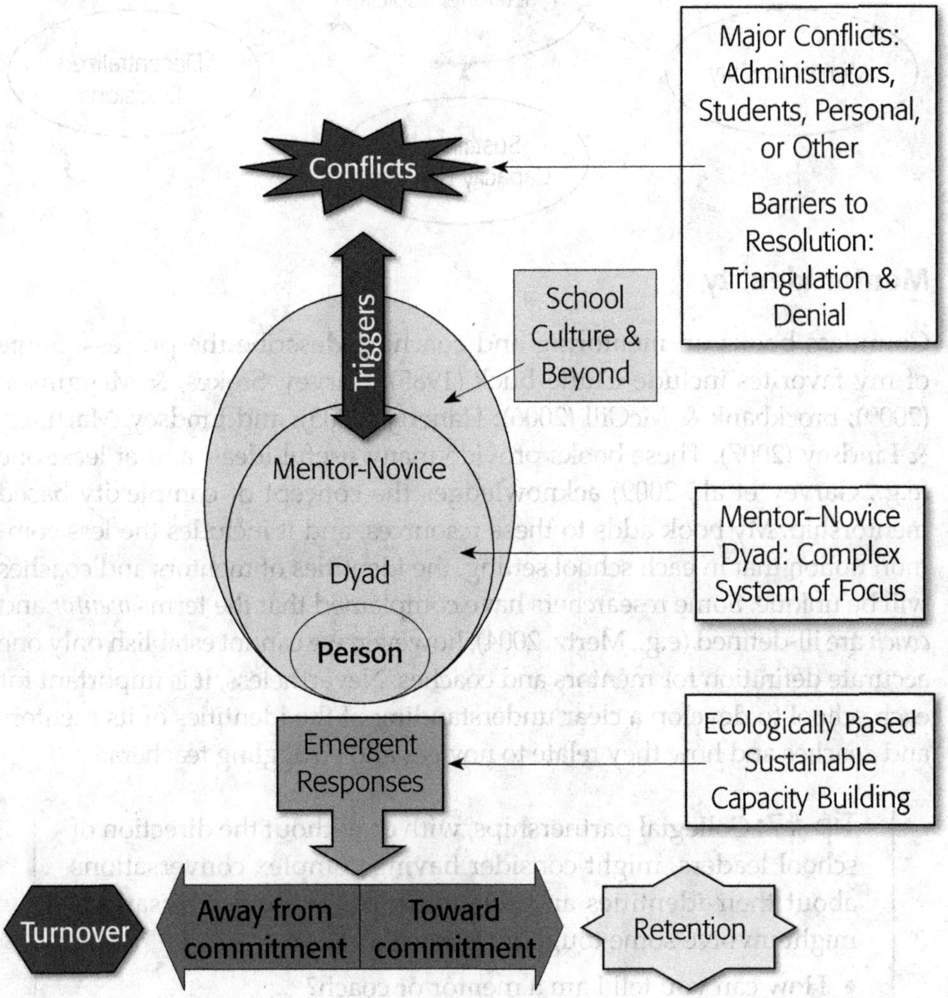

Implications for Practitioners

In my study, I also discovered some ideas that could be of help to those who are involved in collegial partnerships. What follows are some explanations and tips that address the following topics: mentor identity, flexibility, redundancy and diversity, decentralized decision-making, and sustainable capacity building. (See Figure 8.3, page 158.)

Figure 8.3 Implications for Practitioners

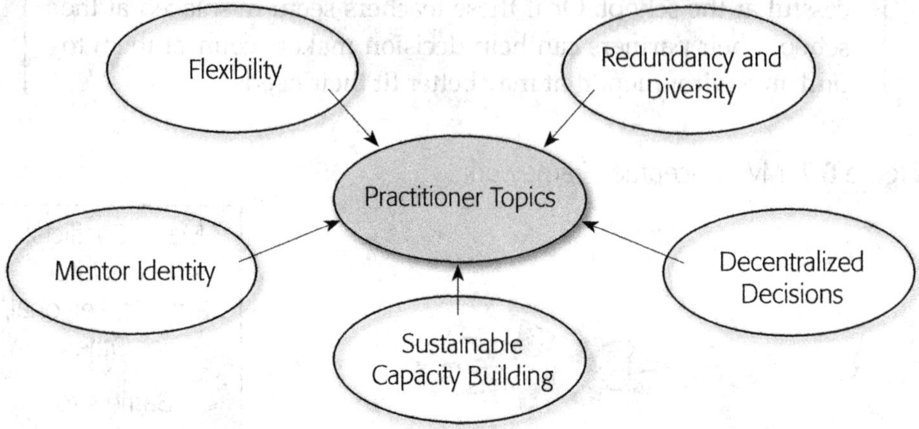

Mentor Identity

Countless books on mentoring and coaching describe the process. Some of my favorites include Clutterbuck (1985); Garvey, Stokes, & Megginson (2009); Brockbank & McGill (2006); Flaherty (2005); and Lindsey, Martinez, & Lindsey (2007). These books provide many useful ideas, and at least one (e.g., Garvey et al., 2009) acknowledges the concept of complexity-based mentorship. My book adds to these resources, and it includes the less common notion that in each school setting, the identities of mentors and coaches will be unique. Some researchers have complained that the terms *mentor* and *coach* are ill-defined (e.g., Mertz, 2004); however, we cannot establish only one accurate definition for mentors and coaches. Nevertheless, it is important for each school to develop a clear understanding of the identities of its mentors and coaches and how they relate to novices and struggling teachers.

Tip #7: Collegial partnerships, with or without the direction of school leaders, might consider having complex conversations about their identities and relationships. These conversations might involve some tough questions:

- How can you tell I am a mentor or coach?
- How can you tell I am a novice or struggling teacher?
- What makes our relationship different from other helping relationships in our school community?
- What can we do if our behaviors change our perceptions of who we say we are in the relationship?

The conversation might also raise many other questions generated by those involved.

Flexibility

I heard the term *flexibility* during one of my first interviews with research participants at Lincoln High School. Most educators understand that flexibility is crucial in schools. Nevertheless, I bring it up here to say that adapting and adjusting in any complex system requires flexibility but also standing firm against forces that would destroy useful values and beliefs. Every person and group can maintain flexible boundaries in order to stay true to themselves and to the work of the group. Being flexible does not mean being indecisive or passive. Both ends of the spectrum of behaviors—passivity and rigidity—could fail in the face of one's practices and relationships.

> **Tip #8:** Mindful collegial partners constantly monitor their responses to each other and to outside systems. In monitoring themselves they might note if their behaviors are tending towards rigidity or passivity. If they find they have moved in either of those directions, and they wish to get back more in balance and toward assertiveness, they may consider having complex conversations with those who are most affected by their behaviors. They may even consider bringing in a trustworthy neutral party to help them determine what happened and how to resolve it. Some questions that might guide the conversation are as follows:
>
> - Are any of us (or either of us) welcoming too many outside or internal influences that go against our fundamental beliefs and values?
> - Are we pushing away new ideas because they go against our fundamental beliefs and values or because they scare us? If they scare us, why is this so?
> - If we are pushing against new ideas, what is our rationale?
>
> An important idea for practitioners to consider about flexibility is that if complex systems do not adapt and change they cease to exist; therefore, even though it is important to stay true to one's self and group, those truths might be constantly examined and in some cases challenged in the light of ever increasing and changing new information.

Redundancy and Diversity

It is critical to understand the interactions of redundancy (similarity) and diversity (difference) if one is going to have a successful collegial partnership. For example, Kalin et al. (2010) suggested that recognizing the value of these opposites is critical to the development of mentorship. The caution about redundancy is that most people want to have comfortable relationships that allow them to be themselves and that avoid unpleasant conflicts. However, based on my findings and the findings of others (e.g., Kalin et al., 2010), it seems highly important for the growth of the individuals and the growth of relationships that diversity play a role. For example, the balance of comfort and challenge is a critical concept for partners to understand and practice.

> **Tip #9:** Mentors and coaches might demonstrate their interest in maintaining relationships based on mutuality by welcoming and respecting the ideas of novices and struggling teachers. Even if these teachers want to look up to them and rely on them for solutions, mentors/coaches must resist the temptation to climb up on the pedestal of admiration from which they proclaim the answers to every challenge these teachers encounter. Novices and struggling teachers can help their collegial partners avoid that pedestal by recognizing their own strengths and capacities to resolve challenges. If partners understand how they co-depend on each other for learning to take place, they may be able to strike a good balance between challenge and support. Practitioners might remember that diversity teaches us respect for each other, and redundancy teaches us that we have strong connections with others to help us endure. It is important for partners to cultivate both of these sides of their relationship.

Decentralized Decisions

A major surprise for me as I was writing this book was that I developed a deeper understanding of the concept of decentralized networks as explained in Davis and Sumara (2006). My understanding of these kinds of networks was that in complex systems, all decisions are made at the level of the system that implements those decisions. What I failed to fully realize is that even though complex systems have short ranges at the level of implementation, they still connect to the central aspect of the network. By remaining connected to the central aspect of the network, they can be robust in terms of the types of solutions available to them, and they can also be efficient in terms of implementing those solutions. The key here is having the best of both hierarchy and mutuality.

> **Tip #10:** If collegial partners and centralized decision makers realize the benefits of hierarchy and mutuality and can understand how to maximize the best of both, they might be able to avoid conflicts created by centralized decisions that do not recognize the importance of local implementation and local implementation that does not recognize the importance of the ideas generated from a centralized or global perspective. Adapting centralized decisions to match the needs of local implementation can be optimal, especially if they are recognized and respected by both elements of the system. For example, when partners find that they need to adjust or adapt a centralized decision to meet the needs of their students or themselves, instead of criticizing the centralized decision making, local practitioners might congratulate themselves for making the best of what they have with the idea of aspiring to achieve the standards determined globally. Rather than criticizing local implementation for adjusting and adapting their standards, centralized decision makers might congratulate them for those adjustments and inquire if they need anything to help them improve. The critical change here is *asking* if they need help, rather than *forcing* that help. The other change is an attitude of appreciation rather than negative and judgmental responses.

Sustainable Capacity Building

Practitioners as well as decision makers might learn the skills of sustainable capacity building as explained by Mitchell and Sackney (2009) and others. They might also consider maintaining an appreciative rather than a deficit perspective that includes never questioning another's competence (Semeniuk & Worrall, 2000). That does not mean that mentors/coaches never question novices/struggling teachers about their practices, but they never question their value as educators. By learning specific skills of communication that facilitate authentic professional dialogue, mentors/coaches and novices/struggling teachers can address all of their challenges.

> **Tip #11:** Mentors or coaches in collaboration with novices or struggling teachers might practice implementing collegial dynamics to help them establish a collaborative culture of

helping based on shared understandings about teaching and learning. They might determine if they are implementing such collegial dynamics as acknowledgment, advocacy, inquiry, and invitation. They might also note if they are open to synchronicity. Finally, collegial partners may determine if they are truly viewing the other as a competent professional. If not, the person who has the negative feelings needs to think carefully about how those feelings emerged. Then, if possible, he or she needs to have an honest conversation with the other person about those feelings to determine if there is a way to change them. If neither person is able to view the other as competent, they need to terminate the relationship.

I have provided several tips that highlight certain ideas that seemed salient in my study and in this book. I think the most important idea is that all educators maintain mutual respect for each other, their students, and everyone involved in the exciting process of learning. If this happens, solutions to challenges are infinite.

References

Barnes, G., Crowe, E., & Schaefer, B. (2007). *The cost of teacher turnover in five school districts: A pilot study*. Retrieved February 15, 2010, from http://www.teachplus.org/uploads/Documents/1292958940_ReadyForTheNextChallenge.pdf.

Block, P. (2008). *Community: The structure of belonging*. San Francisco, CA: Barrett-Koehler Publishers.

Bohm, D. (1980). *Wholeness and the implicate order*. London: Routledge & Kegan Paul.

Bonner Curriculum. (n.d.). *Identity circles: A personal exploration of diversity*. Retrieved February 11, 2012, from http://www.youthgrantmakers.org/wp-content/uploads/2010/07/Diversity-and-Inclusion-Toolkit-Teachers-Edition.pdf.

Bowen, M. (1978). *Family therapy in clinical practice*. New York, NY: Jason Aronson, Inc.

Brockbank, A., & McGill, I. (2006). *Facilitating reflective learning through mentoring & coaching*. Philadelphia, PA: Kogan Page.

Capra, F. (2002). *The hidden connections: Integrating the biological, cognitive, and social dimensions of life into a science of sustainability*. New York: Doubleday.

Cary, L. (2004). The professional development school model: Unpacking knowledge. *International Journal of Leadership in Education, 7*(4), 319–337.

Cincinnati Public Schools. (2006). Pyramid of interventions: Quick guide. Retrieved May 3, 2012, from http://cps-k12.org/general/Pyramid/QuickGuide.pdf.

Clutterbuck, D. (2004). *Everyone needs a mentor: Fostering talent in your organization* (4th ed.). London, UK: Chartered Institute of Personnel and Development.

Cooperrider, D., Whitney, D., & Stavros, J. (2007). *Appreciative inquiry handbook*. San Francisco, CA: Berrett-Koehler.

Davis, B., & Sumara, D. (2006). *Complexity and education: Inquiries into learning, teaching, and research*. Mahwah, NJ: Lawrence Erlbaum Associates, Publishers.

Daye, D. (n.d.) *Branding Strategy Insider: The Branding Blog* Retrieved February 15, 2012, from http://brandingstrategyinsider.com/.

Denning, S. (2004). *Squirrel inc.: A fable of leadership through storytelling*. San Francisco, CA: Jossey-Bass.

Diversity and Dialogue. (n.d.). *Communication and trust-building exercises*. Retrieved August 10, 2012, from http://diversityanddialogue.org.uk/files/communication_activities_0.pdf.

DuFour, R., & Eaker, R. (1998). *Professional learning communities at work: Best practices for enhancing student achievement*. Alexandria, VA: Association for Supervision and Curriculum Development.

Eaker, R., DuFour, R., & DuFour, R. (2002). *Getting started: Reculturing schools to become professional learning communities*. Bloomington, IN: National Educational Service.

Eisely, L. (1969). The starfish story. Retrieved June 16, 2011, from http://www.starbrite.com/starfish.html.

Father Heart Ministries. (2010). Small groups: Relationship builders for small groups. *Tools for mentoring*. Retrieved August 8, 2012, from http://toolsformentoring.com/small-group/relationship-builders.html.

Flaherty, J. (2005). *Coaching: Evoking excellence in others* (2nd ed.). New York, NY: Elsevier.

Garvey, R., Stokes, P., & Megginson, D. (2009). *Coaching and mentoring: Theory and practice*. Los Angeles, CA: Sage.

Gold, Y. (1996) Beginning teacher support: Attrition, mentoring and induction. In J. Sikula (Ed.), *Handbook of research on teacher education* (2nd ed.) (pp. 548–594). New York, NY: Macmillan Publishing Company.

Guarino, C., Santibanez, L., & Daley, G. (2006). Teacher recruitment and retention: A review of the recent empirical literature. *Review of Educational Research, 76*, 173–208.

Hargreaves, A. (2002). Teaching and betrayal. *Teachers and teaching: theory and practice, 8*(3/4), 393–407.

Hargreaves, A., & Dawe, R. (1990). Paths of professional development: Contrived collegiality, collaborative culture, and the case of peer coaching. *Teaching and Teacher Education, 6*(3), 227–241.

Himmellman, A. (1994). Communities working collaboratively for change. In M. Herrman (Ed.), *Resolving conflict: Strategies for local government* (pp. 27–47). Washington, DC: International City/County Management Association.

Himmelman, A. (2001). On coalitions and the transformation of power relations: Collaborative betterment and collaborative empowerment. *American Journal of Community Psychology, 29*(2), pp. 277–285.

Ingersoll, R. (2002). *Who controls teachers' work? Power and accountability in America's schools*. Cambridge, MA: Harvard University Press.

Isaacs, W. (1999). *Dialogue and the art of thinking together*. New York, NY: Currency.

Jaworski, J. (1996). *Synchronicity: The inner path of leadership*. San Francisco, CA: Berrett-Koehler.

Johnson, S. (1998). *Who moved my cheese?* New York, NY: G. P. Putnam's Sons.

Joyce, B., & Showers, B. (1983). *Power in staff development through research in training*. Alexandria, VA: Association of Supervision and Curriculum Development.

Jung, C. (1960). Synchronicity: An acausal connecting principle (R. Hull, trans.). In C. Jung, *The structure and dynamics of the psyche, Vol.8* of *The collected works of C. G. Jung*. Princeton, NJ: Princeton University Press.

Kram, K. (1988). *Mentoring at work: Developmental relationships in organizational life*. Lanham, MD: University Press of America, Inc.

Kalin, N., Barney, D., & Irwin, R. (2010). Complexity thinking mentorship: An emergent pedagogy of graduate research development. *Mentoring and Tutoring: Partnership in Learning, 17*(3), 353–367.

Ladyshewsky, R. (2006). Peer coaching: A constructivist methodology for enhancing critical thinking in postgraduate business education. *Higher Education Research & Development, 25*(1), 67–84.

Lave, J., & Wenger, E. (1991). *Situated learning.* Cambridge, UK: Cambridge University Press.

Lee, F. (1997). When the going gets tough, do the tough ask for help? Help seeking and power motivation in organization. *Organizational Behavior and Human Decision Processes, 72*(3), 336–363.

Lindsey, D., Martinez, R., & Lindsey, R. (2007). *Culturally proficient coaching: Supporting educators to create equitable schools.* Thousand Oaks, CA: Corwin Press.

Meadows, D. (n.d.). Why would anyone want to play starpower? Retrieved February 15, 2012, from http://sustainer.org/dhm_archive/index.php?display_article=vn151starpowered.

Mertz, N. (2004). What's a mentor anyway? *Educational Administration Quarterly, 40*(4), 541–560.

Mitchell, C., & Sackney, L. (2001). Building capacity for a learning community. *Canadian Journal of Educational Administration and Policy, 19,* 1–10. Retrieved February 10, 2009, from http://umanitoba.ca/publications/cjeap/articles/mitchellandsackney.html.

Mitchell, C., & Sackney, L. (2009). *Sustainable improvement: Building learning communities that endure.* Rotterdam, Netherlands: Sense Publishers.

National Center for Education Statistics. (2010). *Teacher attrition and mobility: Results from the 2008–2009 teacher follow-up survey.* Retrieved October 12, 2010, from http://nces.ed.gov/pubs2010/2010353.pdf.

National Commission on Teaching and America's Future (NCTAF) and NCTAF State Partners. (2002). *Unraveling the "teacher shortage" problem: Teacher retention is the key.* Washington, DC. Retrieved December 26, 2011, from http://ncsu.edu/mentorjunction/text_files/teacher_retentionsymposium.pdf.

Noddings, N. (2005). *The challenge to care in schools: An alternative approach to education* (2nd ed.). New York, NY: Teachers College Press.

Northey, S. S. (2005). *Handbook on Differentiating Instruction in Middle and High School.* Larchmont, NY: Eye On Education.

PR Newswire. (2012). *Standardized testing pros and cons: Latest research analyzed on new ProCon.org website.* Retrieved August 10, 2012, from http://prnewswire.com/news-releases/standardized-testing-pros-and-cons-latest-research-analyzed-on-new-proconorg-website-124366098.html.

Pratt, S. (2008). Complex constructivism: Rethinking the power dynamics of "understanding." *Journal of the Canadian Association for Curriculum Studies, 6*(1), pp. 113–132.

Prigogine, I., & Stengers, I. (1984). Order out of chaos. New York: Bantam.

Richardson, J. (2004). Lesson study: Teachers learn how to improve instruction. *National Staff Development Council.* Retrieved April 27, 2012, from http://nsdc.org/members/tools/tools2-04.pdf.

Semeniuk, A., & Worrall, A. (2000). Rereading the dominant narrative of mentoring. *Curriculum Inquiry, 30*(4), 405–428.

Senge, P., Scharmer, C., Jaworski, J., & Fowers, S. (2004). *Presence: Exploring profound change in people, organizations, and society.* New York, NY: Society for Organizational Learning.

Silver, H. F., Strong, R. W., & Perini, M. J. (2000). *So each may learn: Integrating learning styles and multiple intelligences.* Alexandria, VA: ASCD.

Simulation Training Systems. (2011). *StarPower*. Retrieved August 8, 2012, from http://stsintl.com/schools-charities/star_power.html.

Stacey, R. (1992). *Managing the unknowable: Strategic boundaries between order and chaos in organizations.* San Francisco, CA: Jossey-Bass.

SurveyMonkey. (2012). Retrieved August 8, 2012, from http://surveymonkey.com/mp/job-satisfaction-survey/.

Terry, L., & Kritsonis, W. (2008). *A national issue: Whether the teacher turnover affects students' academic performance?* Retrieved July 12, 2012, from http://eric.ed.gov/PDFS/ED499543.pdf.

Tom Wolff & Associates. (2005). *Collaborative solutions: True collaboration as the most productive form of change.* Retrieved May 24, 2012, from http://tomwolff.com/collaborative-solutions-newsletter-summer-05.htm.

Waterman, R. (1987). *The renewal factor: How to best get and keep the competitive edge.* New York: Bantam Books.

Waterman, S. S. (2005). *Handbook on differentiated instruction for middle and high schools.* Larchmont, NY: Eye On Education.

Waterman, S. (2007). *The democratic differentiated classroom.* Larchmont, NY: Eye On Education.

Waterman, S. (2009a). *Differentiating assessment in middle and high school mathematics and science.* Larchmont, NY: Eye On Education.

Waterman, S. (2009b). *Differentiating assessment in middle and high school English and social studies.* Larchmont, NY: Eye On Education.

Waterman, S. (2010a). *Assessing middle and high school mathematics and science: Differentiating formative assessment.* Larchmont, NY: Eye On Education.

Waterman, S. (2010b). *Assessing middle and high school social studies and English: Differentiating formative assessment.* Larchmont, NY: Eye On Education.

Waterman, S. (2012). *Using a complexity-based perspective to better understand the relationships among mentoring, school conflicts, and novice retention.* (Doctoral dissertation). Retrieved from ProQuest LLC (UMI NO. 3490581).

Waterman, S., & He, Y. (2011). Effects of mentoring on new teacher retention: A review of the literature. *Mentoring and Tutoring: Partnership in Learning, 19*(2), 139–156.

Weick, K. (1976). Educational organizations as loosely coupled systems. *Administrative Science Quarterly, 21*(1), 1–19.

Wheatley, M. (2006). *Leadership and the new science: Discovering order in a chaotic world.* San Francisco, CA: Berrett-Koehler.

Wilderdom. (2009). *Trust building activities.* Retrieved August 10, 2012, from http://wilderdom.com/games/TrustActivities.html.

Wong, H. (2005). *The first days of school.* Sunnyvale, CA: Harry K. Wong Publishing Co.

9781596672307